Beyond the Acropolis

BEYOND
THE
ACROPOLIS
·

A Rural Greek Past

Tjeerd H. van Andel
Curtis Runnels

Stanford University Press 1987
Stanford, California

Stanford University Press
Stanford, California
© 1987 by the Board of
Trustees of the
Leland Stanford
Junior University

Printed in the United
States of America

CIP data appear at the end
of the book

Preface

In the history of Western civilization Greece has played a role greatly out of proportion to its size and power. Its inhabitants have never been numerous, nor noted for the ability to impose their will for long beyond the boundaries of their homeland, as the Persians and Romans did so well. Yet in antiquity, Greek thought, art, skills, and goods were valued from Spain to India and from central Europe to Egypt, and their cultural influence remained long after greater military and administrative powers had come and gone again. Greek architectural styles are reflected in innumerable courthouses, banks, and monuments across the Western world. Greek theater effortlessly transcends 2,500 years, as anyone who has sat through a play by Sophocles can testify. Greek philosophy, especially in its rational approach to nature, continues to inform Western science and the humanities. Finally, although democracy today is very different from that of Athens in the fifth century B.C., its ancient roots are always recognized, and any occasional misgivings we might have about it were anticipated by Plato, who felt that "democracy gives equality to the equal and unequal alike."

Today's Greece offers the thoughtful traveler more than its translucent scenery, ancient ruins, and lively tavernas. A few summers ago, out in the hot countryside, we were invited in for water, fruit, and a little talk by an elderly farm couple, as so often happens in this generous and conversation-loving country. Discovering that they had recently visited a married daughter in Philadelphia, one of us asked whether they intended to move to the United States, there to live in American comfort near their child. At this, the old man swung wide the curtain across the doorway, saying, somewhat dramatically, "You drank my water; wasn't it fresh? You ate my melon and my peaches; weren't they sweet? Is not my view grand over this beautiful country? When winter comes, can I not go home to the village to sit in the square talking to my friends? Why should I move to America?" The experience left us quite bemused.

An impressive array of monuments, art works, writings, and excavations still exists today for us to assess the dimensions of ancient Greek civilization. The high culture of the Greeks has been discussed in scholarly texts and coffee table books, seen by millions of tourists, exploited in doctoral dissertations by a hundred generations of students, and taught in innumerable classes. Few are those who do not have some image, however modest, of our Greek heritage, and yet, we do not know why it was just this people that had such an extraordinary influence on the course of civilization. We must also not forget that civilization does not exist by high culture alone: commerce must flourish, and ships must sail to remote places; artists and philosophers must eat; and cities depend on the countryside, where farmers farm and shepherds tend to their flocks. Yet we hear little about rural Greece, so little that it is more than just surprising; it is unacceptable.

One of the first to recognize the need for research on ancient rural Greece was Michael H. Jameson, then Professor of Classics at the University of Pennsylvania. In the 1950's he began a series of explorations of the southern Argolid, a remote tip of the eastern Peloponnese, explorations that eventually led to collaboration with Professor Thomas W. Jacobsen of Indiana University on major excavations of the Archaic and Classical city of Halieis and of the prehistoric deposits of Franchthi cave. Full reports on these excavations have yet to appear; where we refer to their findings in subsequent chapters we have used only material already published, as cited in the Bibliography.

To set these excavations in a regional context, in 1972 Jameson and Jacobsen undertook a systematic archaeological survey of the surroundings of the Franchthi cave. This survey confirmed the archaeological richness of the area and the promise of a survey approach, and demonstrated the need for a longer and more interdisciplinary study in which the evolution of the landscape would be given equal weight with the history of its cultures. Jameson moved to Stanford in 1976, where he found in van Andel a common interest in and a shared perception of this task. Warmly supported by a number of Stanford alumni, the Argolid Exploration Project was continued by a Stanford team beginning in 1979. The archaeological survey has now come to an end, and a comprehensive report is in preparation (M. H. Jameson, C. N. Runnels, and Tj. H. van Andel, *The Southern Argolid: A Greek Countryside from Prehistory to the Present Day*, Stanford University Press, forthcoming).

The results of the project have exceeded our expectations and would, we believe, interest an audience wider than one of archaeologists concerned professionally with Greece. This little book is intended for all who are interested in Greece and its role in history and civilization, and we hope that its reading will enhance their understanding and also provide some pleasure, as the writing of it has done for us. Throughout we have tried to make clear how we attempted to reason from our often multifarious evidence to sometimes bold conclusions. The perspective we present is at times personal in the choice of what we display from the rich yield of the study and in the manner in which we set forth our interpretations. Others might have chosen or argued differently or more cautiously, or would have provided more substantial evidence. For them is intended the larger work, in which the scholarly trappings and footnotes can be found that we have omitted here for the benefit of the general reader. At the end of the present book we have added both a bibliographic essay, which contains recommendations for further general reading and references by chapter, and a bibliography to aid those readers who wish to evaluate in greater depth the basis for our reasoning.

The range of studies underlying this book is broad, and the number of co-workers to whom we owe thanks is larger than we can mention here, but without Thomas Boyd, Hamish Forbes, Timothy Gregory, Nick Kardulias, Susan Langdon, Mark and Mary Lou Munn, Kevin Pope, Daniel Pullen, Jeremy Rutter, Mark Sheehan, and Susan and Robert Sutton, what has been achieved would have been impossible. Without Michael H. Jameson, co-director of the project, it would never even have begun; his insight has been evident and pervasive throughout the study, as it will continue to be in all of its publications. Long conversations with Thomas W. Jacobsen, director of the Franchthi excavation, and with members of his team, including William R. Farrand, Julie Hansen, Sebastian Payne, and especially Catherine Perlès and Judith Shackleton, have greatly stimulated our thinking. We have been careful, however, to rely here only on published material and must assume sole responsibility for the conclusions we have drawn. Very special thanks we owe to Priscilla Murray, who did the sketches of landscapes, villages, and a few of our finds, which make such a lively contrast with the more formal text figures and, we hope, will provide a flavor of the land where we worked.

We are indebted to the Archaeological Service of the Greek Ministry of Culture and Science, especially to members of the Navplion Ephorate of Prehistoric and Classical Archaeology, who are responsible for the administration of the Argolid, and to the director of the Institute of Geology and Mineral Exploration in Athens, who permitted us to carry out the study. The National Endowment for the Humanities, the National Science Foundation, the National Geographic Society, and numerous Stanford alumni and alumnae made the project financially possible and so permitted many undergraduate and graduate students to participate in it. To all we express here our deepest gratitude.

Stanford University   Tj. H. v. A.
July 1986   C. R.

Contents

Tables, Maps, and Figures

FIGURES

Beyond the Acropolis

Introduction

•

Bright Dots on a
Shadowed Landscape

Standing on the Athenian Acropolis, one finds the ancient city packed close around the base of the rock, with modern additions flung east, south, and west. Behind, to the north, rise the barren slopes of Mount Hymettus and Mount Pendeli; to the right are the far silhouette of the Parnis range and the valley of the Kephisos leading into inner Attica, an open country of limestone ridges and valleys, as sparsely settled now as it was during the Classical period.

This is Greece, thinly populated except where people have gathered together in villages and a few towns. To the ancient Greeks only their towns and some famous sanctuaries outside them were of any interest. The countryside is rarely mentioned and never specifically described. The following sketch reflects our modern appreciation of the charms of the Greek landscape, but few Greeks of ancient times would have thought this worth recording: "Between the last view of Athens and the first view of the Bay of Salamis there lies on the Sacred Way a stretch of almost level road. Here the hills shut in the pass to north and south. The pines grow thicker, the narrow stretch of grass by the road widens to an English greensward across which the wooded slopes of Mount Aegaleus make a deep shadow." (R. C. Bosquet, *Days in Attica*.)

Even when the ancient Greeks expressed an appreciation of nature, it often took on a rather practical overtone. Sappho, admiring the landscape, chose a special case when she wrote, "The cornland glows with light upon its thousand blooms," suggesting, incidentally, that weed control was even then a problem; and Sophocles likewise, when he described nature's most useful gift to the Greeks: "On these plains, our sweet grey foster nurse the olive grows." Hesiod, in his *Works and Days* (eighth century B.C.), most pragmatically describes the seasons of the farmer, but in terms so general that we fail to recognize the landscape even though we know where he lived.

Pausanias, in his *Guide to Greece* (a second century A.D. travel guide), went straight from town to sanctuary to town, keeping silent until he arrived at the next center of civilization. Through our imagination, consequently, we must fill with farms, hamlets, or villages the apparent emptiness of the ancient Greek countryside, because we are seldom given an inkling of their existence, let alone of their appearance. For most ancient Greeks the countryside merely served to separate one town from another.

It is therefore no surprise that ancient accounts do not inform us particularly well about rural Greece, its geography, its economics, and its history; and archaeologists have not been of much help, either. Except for a small number of regional surveys, they have preferred to excavate temples, a stadium, or a Mycenaean palace rather than a farm or a rural village. Their preference is understandable, and it is reinforced by the equally understandable desire of their financial sponsors to attach their names to the excavation of a famous tomb rather than that of a country hamlet. As a result, however, we search the literature, both ancient and modern, mostly in vain to find what agricultural reality lay behind Greek high culture. It is to help fill this gap that the study that we describe in the following chapters was undertaken.

Since the later Bronze Age, Greek farming has emphasized the characteristic Mediterranean triad of wheat, wine, and olives, supplemented by the herding of sheep and goats. Although in some parts of the country cattle and pigs are and have been raised, in summer most of Greece is too dry to provide the fodder and water to make this a useful practice. Even today, pastoralism ranges from the local grazing of small flocks to long travels on foot between summer pastures in the high mountains of Epiros and Arkadia, and winter grazing in the fallow fields of the lowlands. Some pastoralists, such as the Vlachs and Sarakatsani, have only recently begun to occupy permanent settlements.

With so little concrete knowledge of the ancient Greek landscape, such ignorance about its rural geography, we do not know even elementary things. Did the Neolithic, Bronze Age, or early historic peasants live in scattered farms, or huddled in villages? Was there some kind of hierarchy to the rural settlement pattern, with farmhouses at the bottom, hamlets next, and regional farm centers at the top? Which lands were used for what purpose? How extensive were farming and herding at one time or another? What were the variations with time in land use, population, types of crops grown, or settlement patterns?

Such ignorance is perhaps to be expected for the early agricultural history in the Neolithic or the following Bronze Age, though the latter has been illuminated brightly, albeit spottily, by the recent decipherment of the Mycenaean Linear B script and the reading of palace archives. It is, however, surprising that our knowledge does not improve much with the onset of the Classical period. In fact, we remain unhappily ignorant well into modern times.

Inevitably, human settlement and human use alter the landscape. The lands of the Mediterranean appear brown, barren, and uninviting, their flora degraded, the soil uncompromising to an eye accustomed to the many shades of green of a more temperate shore. Deep soils, dense vegetation, and rich arable lands are restricted to valley bottoms and coastal plains, whereas the mountains everywhere are rocky, eroded, and barely good enough for goats. The barrenness of the Greek landscape, viewed with disapproval by visitors from lusher parts, who regard it as underused and most likely badly mismanaged, drew early comment. Plato said that "previously the plains of Phelleus were full of rich soil, and there were many woods on the mountains, of which signs can still been seen. For some of the mountains will now support only bees, but not so long ago trees were cut from thence for roofing the largest buildings. In all places there flowed abundant streams of springs and rivers." (*Kritias* III.) It is worth remembering, however, that he referred to a mythical Attica 9,000 years before his time and before an also mythical great deluge. More realistic, and very much to the point of our discourse, is what Aristotle noted about the plain of Argos: "In the time of the Trojan War, Argos was marshy and able to support few inhabitants only, while Mycenae was good land and the more famous. Now the opposite is the case. Mycenae has become unproductive and completely dry, while the Argive land that was once marshy and unproductive is under cultivation. What has happened in this small district may therefore be supposed to happen to large districts and whole countries. Those whose vision is limited think that the cause of these effects is a universal process of change, the whole universe being in the process of growth. . . . There is some truth to this, but some falsehood also." (*Meteorologia* I, 14.)

These and other statements by ancient authors have strengthened in some the conviction that Greece must once have been well watered and wooded but was degraded by man, mostly during the days of Greece's greatest glory in the last millennium B.C. and the early centuries A.D., through soil erosion, overgrazing, and deforestation for fuel and timber. Modern scholars especially seem to favor grand estimates of the amount of forest felled to build ships for the naval wars of the Classical, Hellenistic, and Roman periods. Such views have been welcomed with approval, even with glee, by environmentalists of the doomsday school who like to hold up the Mediterranean as a particularly gruesome example of the consequences of overpopulation and of our cavalier attitude toward nature.

The evidence for all this, however, is slim. The ancient authors, when describing the lushness of the Greek landscape, refer to a mythical past they themselves never saw. Their refusal to be specific about the landscape makes it impossible to judge precisely how much more extensive deep soils and woodland were then than now. Nor do estimates of the amount of timber

Map 1. Greece and the southern Argolid, with principal place names used in the text.

felled for shipbuilding take account of the potential for regrowth, which is actually quite high for such trees as the Mediterranean pine and oak, even with minimal care. Russell Meiggs has argued persuasively that large-scale deforestation actually came to the Mediterranean quite late, in the nineteenth and the early twentieth century, for the simple reason that until the advent of railroads the means were lacking to transport timber over large distances from the mountains to cities and shores. Unanswered remains the question to what degree grazing and woodcutting for fuel have degraded the Mediterranean forests over the centuries. Moreover, the evidence, so far as it goes, indicates that whatever major deforestation took place in Greece by human hand cannot be laid at the door of Classical and later Greece but must in the main be relegated to a much earlier time, probably five to six millennia ago. Since then a new, complex, interesting, and, in its own right, beautiful vegetation has evolved, the low, shrubby maquis, inadequately appreciated by tourists who see only its brown summer state, and not the flowering glory of its spring. This very same maquis now covering the slopes, if left alone for just a few decades, quite easily regenerates into scrubby woodland. Greek history records many an occasion when economic decline or depopulation provided just such a pause to refresh the land.

The following, then, are the questions that led Michael Jameson, together with us and others, to devise the southern Argolid project. What was the distribution of dwelling sites and settlements from the moment the first human beings set foot in the area, and how did their size and pattern vary with time? What were the opportunities offered settlers in the region by its natural environment, or, conversely, how did the environment restrict human occupation? What lands were used for which purpose? How did nature affect settlement, and, in turn, how did settlement alter natural conditions? As G. P. Marsh, a nineteenth century American geographer, wrote, perhaps too pessimistically, in his *Man and Nature*, "Man is everywhere a disturbing agent. Wherever he plants his foot, the harmonies of nature are turned to discord."

What were the functions of the various kinds of sites, and did they reflect some sort of economic or political hierarchy from farmstead and hamlet to country town and city? Do site numbers and site patterns reliably reflect the vagaries and vicissitudes of the rural economy and the population density of

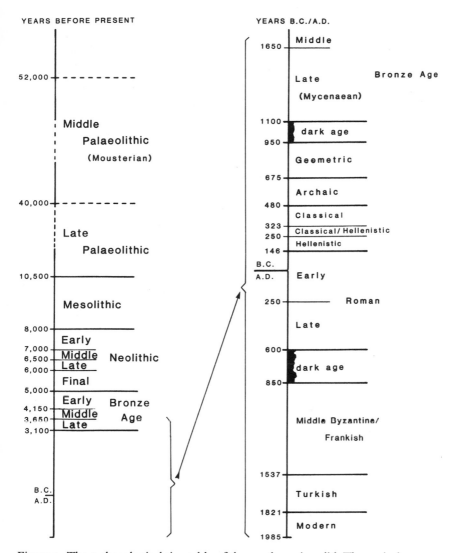

YEARS BEFORE PRESENT

YEARS B.C./A.D.

	1650 — Middle
52,000 — – – – – – – – –	Late Bronze Age
	(Mycenaean)
Middle	1100 —
Palaeolithic	dark age
(Mousterian)	950 —
	Geometric
	675 —
	Archaic
40,000 — – – – – – – – –	480 —
	Classical
Late	323 — Classical/Hellenistic
	250 —
Palaeolithic	Hellenistic
	146 —
	B.C.
10,500 —	A.D. — Early
	250 — Roman
Mesolithic	Late
8,000 —	
Early	600 —
7,000 — Middle Neolithic	dark age
6,500 — Late	
6,000 —	850 —
Final	
5,000 —	
Early Bronze	Middle Byzantine/
4,150 — Middle Age	Frankish
3,650 — Late	
3,100 —	
	1537 —
B.C.	Turkish
A.D.	1821 —
	Modern
	1985 —

Figure 1. The archaeological timetable of the southern Argolid. The period names and chronological boundaries are widely used, but it should be understood that somewhat different period names and dates are accepted by some other scholars. Because they are more easily retained this way, we have chosen to label the historic boundaries with specific years rather than with general designations such as "middle of the third century B.C." Those boundaries, of course, are never sharp and were invisible to the people living at the time. (We note that in the text we have capitalized the first letter of "early," "middle," and "late" when an event or site could be firmly assigned to a period so designated in the chart. Without an initial capital, these words are merely adjectives referring to an early, middle, or late part of a period; "early Roman" can thus be understood as "early in the Roman period.")

the southern Argolid? And finally, how do the local economy and population density relate to or depend on the political and economic history of the Aegean and the Mediterranean?

All this, of course, leaves unanswered two wider questions: Can what we have learned in the southern Argolid be taken to have meaning for the rest of Greece, and can we absolve man, as Oliver Rackham has suggested, of most of the blame for the barrenness of the Greek landscape? Clearly, we shall be unable to answer either of these in full, but a beginning must be made somewhere. Thoughtful people will have to provide their own extrapolations.

We should have preferred to ask these questions of all of Greece, to be sure of the validity of the answers, but that was patently impossible; it would take either a lifetime of work by ourselves or a slightly shorter period with an army of investigators. Thus, the exploration of the southern Argolid is merely one small contribution to a debate that will continue as the evidence grows. What the southern Argolid is and was like, why it was chosen, and how it was explored, are the subjects of the next two chapters.

Chapter 1

•

A Greek Countryside

The Argolid, easternmost of the four fingers of the Peloponnese, consists, outside the famous plain of Argos, mainly of mountain country. Known in antiquity as the Akte, the region lacks the soaring heights and sharp, snow-covered peaks of the Parnon and Taygetos ranges of the Peloponnesian mainland, but more than one-third of it lies above six hundred meters, and several summits exceed a thousand. Commonly the mountains descend directly into the sea, and coastal plains are few and small. Consequently, access from the sea is limited to a few safe landfalls, such as the excellent harbors of Koiladha, Porto Kheli, and Ermioni.

Nor is it much easier to travel overland. The peninsula has a marked east-to-west cross grain. Its many transverse mountains are separated by narrow valleys and gorges that descend to the sea toward either the east or the west but rarely provide a convenient pathway from one coast to the other. Epidauros, famed for its sanctuary of Asklepios and its wonderful theater, is the sole exception; it straddles a valley that connects the rich Argive plain in the west with a harbor on the northeastern shore, opposite Attica. The high country ends at the major Dhidhima and Adheres ranges, the northern border of the area of our studies, the tip of the Akte, the southern Argolid.

Three main political units, defined largely by topographic barriers and by the rare convenient points of access, form of old the Akte; they coincide approximately with the territories of three Classical city-states. In the north lies the Epidauria,

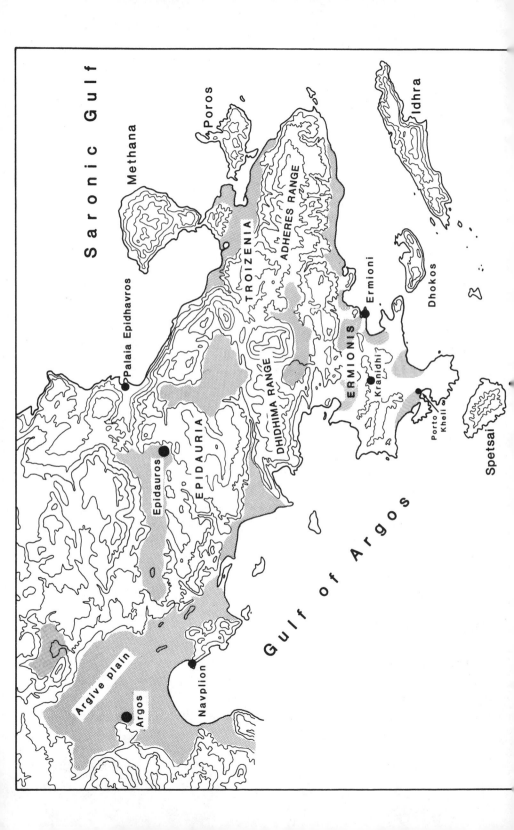

centered on the Asklepios sanctuary and on the route from the plain of Argos to the small but safe port at Palaia Epidhavros, on the Saronic Gulf. The eastern portion forms the Troizenia, the old city of Troizen at its center, with a political and economic orientation toward the north and Attica. Tucked away south of the formidable Dhidhima and Adheres ranges is the isolated Ermionis with its ancient city of Hermion (now Ermioni), sometimes independent, at other times looking toward Argos. Finally, a small, geographically ill-defined city-state existed between about 750 and 280 B.C. at Halieis, on the bay of Porto Kheli in the extreme south.

The mountains of the Akte, though round and not much dissected, are steep and high, with sparse vegetation good only for grazing. Only the easternmost tip, the Adheres range, betrays by its intricate relief of deep, steep-flanked valleys a softer bedrock of shales and sandstones.

Different from the rest of the Akte is its extreme southern tip, the south half of the area of our study. Underlain by very much younger, soft, easily eroded marls and shales, it consists of gently rolling hills not higher than 100 m and traversed by steep-sided stream valleys. Originally, many of the hills were covered with deep and fertile soil, the mainstay of early agriculture, of which remnants can be found to this day.

Coastal plains are rare. The largest by far is the Argive plain, which, through its several major streams, is actively building out into the northern Gulf of Argos. Smaller plains fringe the Troizenia and the shore opposite the island of Idhra. They are also found inside the embayments of the scalloped south coast. In the main, however, the Akte is a land of mountains, not of plains; at the present time plains and valley floors occupy less than 20 percent of its surface.

The climate of the southern Argolid is typically Mediterranean; it rains almost exclusively in the fall and winter months, and the summers, except for an occasional thunderstorm, are

Map 2 (facing page). The mountainous Argolid peninsula, from the Argive plain to its southern edge. Its relief is indicated with contour lines at 100, 200, 400, 600, 800, and 1,000 m; plains and upland plateaus are shaded.

clear and dry. The 500 mm of annual precipitation, which would be regarded as middling in coastal California, come down on a relatively small number of rainy days. The winter is therefore mostly sunny, the days pleasant though not warm. Snow falls at times in the higher mountains, but the lower levels never see it. The summers, on the other hand, can be hot indeed, especially in the interior.

The rain falling on the limestone mountains, rather than running off on the surface, works its way down through cracks and fissures, and has over millions of years created a network of subterranean channels betrayed here and there by caves. Where these channels reach an impermeable level (shale, for example, or the ubiquitous dense igneous rocks, the ophiolites) they follow it until they exit through a line of springs along an outcropping contact between permeable and impervious rock formations. Although many have dried up recently as a result of excessive pumping of innumerable wells, springs were once common, and some still flow copiously even today. Only on the less permeable shales of the Adheres range is surface runoff common, but even there it does not usually last much past the spring. Understandably, permanent streams are rare and mainly found in the upper and middle valleys. Only here and there, in some of the inland basins and plateaus, does one encounter as late as August or September the pleasant sight of water trickling down a small brook under pink flowering oleanders and spreading plane trees.

The mountain slopes are clad in maquis, a dense brush of junipers, shrubby, prickly evergreen oak, and locally wild olive, with thorny shrublets of great variety and much spring splendor of bloom. The soft yellowish green of pine woods is commonly seen on coastal slopes, where their resin is harvested as a preservative for the Greek wine retsina, an acquired taste. Olive groves everywhere climb the lower slopes on soil carefully retained behind stone terrace walls.

For thousands of years, cereal agriculture on the deep soils of the inland basins and valleys and on the rolling hills and coastal plains of the extreme south has been the substance of life here. In times of population growth it expanded onto the lower slopes and river terraces, usually together with the cultivation of the olive. In times of decline the poorer, stonier, and steeper fields tended to be abandoned or left to the olive, a tree that is satisfied with little moisture and a less fertile soil. Vineyards exist today and probably since the Late Bronze Age, but their economic role is limited and mainly local.

It is a tranquil landscape, neither lush nor barren, rounded rather than precipitous, the wide valleys a mosaic of blond grain fields and silver olive groves between the green-flecked white of the limestone ridges. The houses cluster in small villages, often perched on a spur or a slope, rather than forming the familiar North American or northwest European pattern of isolated farms centered efficiently on the family land. In modern Greece, property ownership is dispersed as a result of centuries of dividing the land for dowries, and a single family's holdings are almost always scattered over a wide area. With such fragmented landholdings, living on one's property is not efficient, and the clustering of dwellings in villages, desirable also for reasons of safety, makes more sense. Has this always been the Greek pattern, and, if so, does highly divided land ownership also go back into more remote times? This is one of the questions that surveys like ours are designed to answer, and we shall return to it later.

As almost everywhere in the Aegean, pastoralism is a perennial part of rural subsistence in the southern Argolid, of greatest importance during times of economic decline, when grazing is the cheapest way to use remote lands of marginal quality. More than half of the Ermionis is still classified as pasturage, and upland villages such as Dhidhima depend much on income from the herding of sheep and goats. Pastoralism is, and long has been, practiced on a local scale, with a few sheep and goats grazing on community lands in one season and in fallow fields in the other, but it also includes transhumance, a farther-flung phenomenon with interesting social and cultural consequences. Transhumance in the Akte involved the seasonal migration of large herds, together with their shepherds and members of their families, from summer pastures high in the mountains of the Peloponnese proper to the winter lowlands of the southern Argolid. It was a fact of Argolid life for thousands of years and survived into recent decades, furnishing besides economic benefits a window on the world beyond the mountains. More recently, the practice has declined, and shepherd communities have settled increasingly among the local population.

There is also the surrounding sea, visible from almost every high point in the Argolid. The sea has provided the area with benefits to supplement subsistence agriculture, but its resources are small here and appear to have been little used in the recent past, the only period of which we have any extensive knowledge. At Franchthi cave, prehistoric deposits bear witness to local fishing and the consumption of shellfish, but today fishing is mainly a part-time occupation during the slack season, when the farm requires little attention. Salt panning also has played its role in the local economy. The lagoon at Thermisi was the site of a lucrative salt industry from at least the late Middle Ages to the nineteenth century, and salt pans existed in Ververonda lagoon, near Porto Kheli, from the seventeenth through the nineteenth century. Whether in Classical times a salt industry gave its name to the city of Halieis remains a matter of debate. Finally, the purple snail (*Murex brandaris*) provided Hermion in its Classical past with a dye industry of some repute.

The sea, of course, furnishes not only resources but also

cheap bulk transportation, important especially before the advent of railways and motor roads. In the southern Argolid, seafaring, most often a blend of service in the merchant marine and local and long distance fishing, has provided a good measure of employment in the recent past and continues to do so today. The independence and wealth of the island of Idhra in the eighteenth and the early nineteenth century, for example, were due to its far-flung commerce by sea, and in the late nineteenth century Kranidhi was still the home of numerous sailors. The successful ones left many a stately house behind in the part of town that lies uphill from the present main road and is thus seldom seen by outsiders. Another sea captain's proud home, this one in the fishing village of Koiladha, opposite Franchthi cave, was later converted to a school and now, having decayed and become unfit for children, it has sheltered our archaeological headquarters for several years.

To depend for one's livelihood upon the sea is precarious. It holds the local economy hostage to the vagaries of a much larger region, and so at times an element of turbulence of external origin is added to the local history. Moreover, not all seafaring is directed toward legitimate gain. Piracy was a constant

problem in Mediterranean maritime affairs until the nineteenth century, and when slaves were a valuable commodity, plundering towns was at least as remunerative as capturing vessels at sea. Under those conditions one expects a withdrawal of settlements to better-concealed or more defensible sites, a phenomenon that can indeed be observed during the region's strife-torn medieval and modern history. Kranidhi, for example, the principal town of the southern Argolid, perched high on a saddle some 4 km away from its harbors at Porto Kheli and Koiladha, is a new town, placed there in Byzantine times with a view more to security than to maritime convenience.

There can be no doubt that the southern Argolid and the Akte as a whole have been able to provide a modest but secure existence for a small population since agriculture was introduced in the area some 8,000 years ago. External forces, varying in mode and intensity with the conditions prevailing in surrounding lands and in the whole eastern Mediterranean, have intermittently forced a more outward orientation on the area, usually resulting in greater prosperity and a larger population. At all times, pastoralism, fishing, and maritime commerce provided a mechanism by which the local population maintained a window on the world. Thus they were able to respond when potential markets for the local cash crop or industry evolved elsewhere, when Argos, Attica, or even more distant parts of the Aegean prospered enough to create a demand that their own surroundings could not satisfy. We shall later discuss ancient examples of this pendulum swing between an orientation toward the outside and a retreat to a more isolated existence, but the present, postwar time furnishes an excellent illustration.

A growing and prospering Athens has for some decades provided a lucrative market for tomatoes, vegetables, citrus, peaches, and apricots, a market that the formerly rather more subsistence-oriented farmers in the Argolid, and in the Argive plain as well, have hastened to supply. Transportation was facilitated when the motor road through the Akte opened up the south, and more recently hydrofoils have brought the southern

Argolid within an hour or two of Athens for weekending Athenians and foreign tourists alike. Enterprising local land speculators have converted much coastal land into innumerable minuscule plots for summer houses, often with lofty disregard for such amenities as water, access, or septic tank drain fields. Success has not invariably followed these enterprises.

Map 3. Relief and principal place names of the southern Argolid. Excavated archaeological sites are marked with stars. Plains and upland plateaus are shaded; hills and mountains are indicated with contours at a 100 m interval. Dashed lines are streams.

In the town of Porto Kheli, twenty years ago little more than a small cluster of houses with anchorage for some fishing boats, there has sprung up a fringe of modern hotels, bars, and discos along the side of the bay opposite the acropolis of ancient Halieis, and tourism has become virtually the sole means of existence of the new town. Elsewhere, large and often isolated seashore hotels, where summer visitors endlessly move between the beach in the daytime and the disco at night, never seeing much of Greece at all, have become major consumers of the vegetables and fruit the region grows and, alas, also of its scarcest commodity, fresh water.

Prosperity based to this extent on tourism is, one assumes, new in the history of the area, but, like any other bonanza dependent on the outside world, it is subject to economic and political fortunes beyond local control. As much as prosperity, however, economic collapse has been a recurring feature of Greek history, and its lessons are well remembered. An elderly couple in Porto Kheli, friends of the archaeologists who have frequented the region for more than twenty years, dwell in a small traditional house behind a large, modern hotel built and managed by their son. During our visits they did not fail to point out with quiet satisfaction that the bread, wine, and olives we consumed were grown on their own land in measure sufficient for their own security, because "hotels come and go, but the land remains." It is a lesson not just Greeks would do well to remember.

In a sense the southern Argolid is an island. Seen by the traveler from automobile or bus, the summer landscape is pleasant enough; the trip from the north to Kranidhi, Porto Kheli, or Ermioni is a brief and charming tour through sunny valleys under the brows of peaceful mountains. The bald peaks, so impressive from a distance, need not be crossed, and the precipitous gorges are mostly hidden from view. Attempt the passage on foot, however, along the short inland route across the Adheres range from Troizen to Ermioni, for example, and the image changes drastically, as there appears to be no end to the steep-walled ravines that must be crossed or the long, arduous slopes to be overcome in the heat haze over the shimmering thorny brush.

We may regard the southern Argolid as an island of a sort, but it is an island tied to the rest of the Peloponnese by seafaring and transhumance. This quality makes the area an excellent choice for our study of the history of rural Greece. When isolated, as for so many of its past millennia, the Argolid was controlled mainly by local conditions, and the essence of its history might be understood from what we can learn about the intertwined evolutions of nature and culture in this small, geographically well defined area. This condition minimizes the great disadvantage facing any pioneer historian, who, beyond the immediate boundaries of his hard-won local information, knows little. Intermittently, on the other hand, the area did open its doors and windows wide to the more prosperous, more powerful, and, in historic times, better recorded periphery. For such times we shall be able to relate the history of the region to the flow of events in a greater and better-known world, something that would not be possible for a truly isolated island or mountain valley. To some satisfactory degree, then, if we just guard against the risk of circular reasoning, we can have it both ways. We can trace the evolution of an isolated area surviving essentially on its own resources during times when greater powers either did not exist or else had no interest in so small and remote a place. For periods of regional prosperity and political consolidation, on the other hand, the southern Argolid would be as useful in considering how the rural infrastructure relates to the historic and economic fate of big cities as if it were located directly in the shadow of the acropolis of Argos or Athens.

The prolonged isolation of the southern Argolid since the Middle Ages and until World War II allowed traditional rural practices to survive into the days when archaeologists and anthropologists became part of the population (at times so highly visible a part that the question was raised whether one should not sponsor an anthropological study of the impact of archaeologists on rural Greece). Hence we have at hand many studies such as those on transhumance along the "thousand year road" between the southern Argolid and the central Peloponnese by Harold Koster, on subsistence agriculture on the isolated slopes of Methana by Hamish Forbes, or on the long-lasting successful cultivation of the olive in the Fournoi valley by Nicolas Gavrielides. The findings of these studies—done in a country so traditional that the 3,500 year old village streets excavated from under the ash of the Santorini volcano, and the houses of medieval Monemvasia in the southern Peloponnese, closely resemble those of tourist-infested Mykonos—are of great help in understanding the past, as we shall illustrate in subsequent chapters.

Naturally, as is true for most research projects, this one was shaped by its own history as much as by design. The wanderings of Michael and Virginia Jameson through the area, begun some 30 years ago, had yielded a rich inventory of architectural remains and less conspicuous sites, as well as a general understanding of the landscape and of what needed doing to illuminate its history in depth. The excavations of Halieis, begun by the Jamesons in 1962 and continued in the 1970's by Wolf Rudolph of Indiana University, and those at Franchthi cave directed since 1967 by Thomas Jacobsen, have provided for the Archaic and Classical periods and for the Stone Age, respectively, a useful and firm anchor. Those at Halieis have also yielded an example of a Roman establishment once also common in Greece that can best be called agribusiness; we later found traces of similar establishments elsewhere in the area. An exploratory survey done in 1972 by Jameson, Jacobsen, and James Dengate of the University of Illinois taught us much about what would or would not be practical, and the continuing work on the finds from Franchthi emphasized the importance of analyzing the evolution of the landscape itself. From these disparate parts was put together the Stanford survey, a joint effort of professionals, graduate student specialists, and successive crews of undergraduates. The excavations of Halieis and Franchthi cave will soon have their own reporters; here we shall describe the archaeological survey and try to discern pattern, rhyme, and reason in the geographic evolution of our region. We shall be guided by and aware of the issues of rural economic history that we have outlined above, but we will not always find ourselves well equipped to deal with them adequately—alas, a common scholarly experience.

Chapter 2

•

Walking in the Fields: Archaeology Without Digging

Almost every human activity in the landscape leaves at least a few traces, no matter how minuscule, but nature and time tend to cover them up until sometimes even the remains of great ancient cities are well concealed. Therefore, any archaeological survey must begin with a simple question, one we have often been asked by students and friends: Where, precisely, does one go to look for archaeological sites, and how does one manage to find them? The question is reasonable in this case because, small as it is, even the southern Argolid contains a vast expanse of mountains, valleys, and plains, too formidable to be searched in its entirety, and one can be excused for wondering how we ever managed to find anything at all.

Our start was somewhat simplified by the fact that there had been two major excavations in the area, one at Halieis, the other at Franchthi. It was natural to begin our investigation with the land around those two so that we might place them in a wider context. On the other hand, substantial areas, now occupied by hotels, roads, towns, factories, and houses, are no longer part of our opportunities, the past there being firmly covered by the present. Even so, more than 200 km² remained to be examined, and that meant a great many, too many, years of exhaustive search on foot for sites of all sizes, functions, and dates. Obviously, to meet our aim of determining patterns of human settlement and land use for every period of the past, we would have to limit the area to be searched and choose it very carefully.

The exploratory survey of 1972 under Jacobsen, Jameson, and Dengate had dealt with the immediate surroundings of the Franchthi cave in the valleys of Fournoi and Koiladha. Although it lasted a mere four weeks, it turned up more than 130 archaeological sites in an area of about 20 km² (ca. 10 percent of the whole area), as well as thousands of artifacts, a surprising and very encouraging result for what was then a new and, in Greece, almost untried archaeological approach.

From that exploratory survey we learned that the countryside, empty as it often seems, was fairly teeming with sites of all ages. Many others must have been destroyed or rendered invisible by the rising sea, by alluvium laid down in valleys, or by human activities ancient and modern. The 1979–83 Stanford survey brought the site total to about 320, but, considering that it only covered an additional 20 percent of the southern Argolid, we can reasonably guess that there may originally have been as many as a thousand sites, even if we allow for a lot of uninhabited rugged mountain country. Extending this to the Akte as a whole, to the Peloponnese, and to all of Greece, we believe that the entire country may once have contained as many as half a million sites. The number discovered by archaeological surveys, to say nothing of excavated sites, is certainly no more than one-tenth of one percent of that. Uncertain as these estimates are, we can say with confidence that since the beginning of the Bronze Age, some 5,000 years ago, Greece has been much lived in, sometimes as much as it is today. The conclusion is also inescapable that so much living must have had an impact on the Greek landscape, even if we remember that those innumerable sites have accumulated gradually over more than 50,000 years and were not all inhabited at the same time.

The Stanford survey did not begin until the summer of 1979, giving us time during the long break after 1972 to learn a great deal from others. The earliest surveys in Greece were directed mainly to the identification of towns and sanctuaries known from the ancient literature. Though very successful in that undertaking, they had not given much attention to the study of patterns and systems of settlement. In other parts of the world, such as Mesopotamia and Central America, surveys had been carried out for some time that were more truly exploratory because they dealt with archaeological *terra incognita*. Their results inspired William McDonald, Richard Hope Simpson, and others to undertake a thorough study of Messenia, in the southwestern Peloponnese, beginning in the 1950's. It was their goal to reconstruct the regional Bronze Age environment, and their results, published in 1972, mark a new era in Greek archaeology. Since then, several others, such as John Cherry for the island of Melos, have shown how remarkable a range of archaeological information can be produced by simple and relatively cheap survey methods without excavation.

Goals and methods were much on our minds when, on Jameson's initiative, we returned to Koiladha in 1979 to begin the work. We had decided to widen the search to include the whole eparchy (county) of the Ermionis, far beyond the boundaries of 1972, and had put together a team to accomplish that goal over a period of about four years. And so each year, until 1983, students from Stanford and other universities, including some from Greece and England, diligently walked the dusty fields of summery Greece, assisted by various archaeological, geological, and anthropological specialists. Yet, even with three field seasons and a crew of twenty, we could not expect to cover more than 10 or 20 percent of the area if we were to be as thorough (and therefore, inevitably, as slow) as seemed necessary to detect even the smallest and most insignificant sites. After considerable thought we decided that our selection had best be guided by the various environments, such as valley floors, steep mountain slopes, or rolling hills, because we could recognize those fairly easily from maps, from field visits, and from the geological study that some of us were doing at the same time. We should have to be certain, however, to include areas where intuition, common sense, or quick inspection told us that conditions were not favorable for human habitation, and where sites therefore might be unlikely to exist. The hills in the Argolid, for example, are often steep,

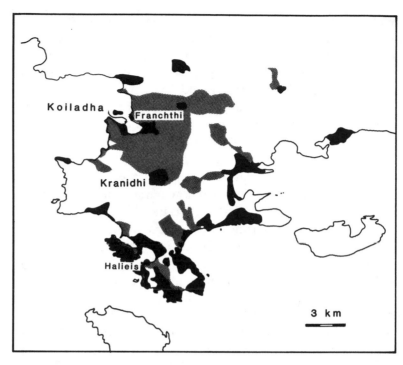

Map 4. Shown here in gray are the areas in the southern Argolid that have
been surveyed in detail. White are the steep, barren mountainsides; they
were not expected and not found to contain many sites, and were visited
more casually. Some areas, appropriately presented in black, were inacces-
sible to us because of buildings, fences, or unsympathetic owners.

their slopes barren and seemingly devoid of archaeological materials, but that would have to be proven, unattractive as the
scramble across steep, empty slopes might be. It was also essential that the areas chosen to be surveyed in detail should be
as representative of the whole as possible, so that at the end we
should be able to apply our conclusions with some confidence
to the entire southern Argolid. Finally, we needed to verify all
sites found during the 1972 survey around Franchthi and in the
Koiladha and Fournoi areas, and to visit those parts that had
been missed that year.

The traverses to be walked were blocked out on topographic

maps to the scale of 1:5,000, made from aerial photographs by the Greek Army Map Service and so accurate and detailed that individual houses, terrace walls, and even single wells were depicted on them. All traverses were then split into two parts, each part to be surveyed separately by a team of five people. One or two of the five were experienced archaeologists; the others, undergraduate students at Stanford with diverse intended careers. Each year from 1979 through 1981 we deployed three teams, then only one in 1982, and 1983 was devoted to checking our results.

During the survey the team members, spaced from 5 to 15 m apart depending on the visibility, would advance in a line, back and forth as if plowing a field, and as much as possible undaunted by fences, trees, or ditches. Daily progress was recorded on the map and in logs, where we noted a great variety of things ranging from team composition, visibility of the soil, and the nature of the terrain to finds of isolated artifacts and ancient features. This is what is known as an intensive survey, designed not to miss even the smallest site, and indeed we found four sites of only 60 to 80 m², and two much smaller than that (one only 12 m²). Obviously, this was sometimes hard work in the hot sun, and very often tedious. Not only did we have to negotiate steep hills and precipitous ravines, or scramble over terrace walls and through thorny hedgerows, but we also faced whole fields of tough thistles often a couple of meters high. Though this may seem an absurd obstacle, those thistles sometimes forced us to skip a field altogether.

It was our purpose to find sites, not artifacts, which were only a means to an end. Sites are, of course, recognized by the artifacts occurring on them, and our definition of a site was accordingly "any location where a concentration of cultural materials with a recognizable boundary was found." Some archaeologists have advocated the recording of all individual finds, but in the southern Argolid, where artifacts occurred for the most part in discrete clusters, this proved unnecessary. Few were found in between; there was little background scatter. In addition, we felt that there should be a recognizable source at each site, where fresh material was found that had until recently been buried or that could still be seen coming out of the ground. This requirement excludes archaeological materials that, for one or another reason, have been dumped far from their original location. Whether a site was large or small, or whatever its function might have been, a single grave or an entire ancient town, made no difference at this stage. A site was a site, and size and function would be considered later, as they will be here also (in Chapter 9).

An archaeological survey, as we found out, is not a means to acquire romantic, valuable, or beautiful objects. For the most part only durable materials such as potsherds, stone tools, brick and tile fragments, or the odd bit of lead or glass survive millennia of burial in the ground or, a worse fate, long exposure at the surface. Occasionally, we found a silver coin or a fragment of a figurine, but such things were all too rare. Yet, the thrill of making an unusual find while picking through the remains on a site thousands of years old made up for much arduous fieldwork, as much for the veteran archaeologist as for the novice student.

One must bear in mind that we could examine only the surface and what lay on it, and that digging even the smallest hole in the most tempting place was not part of our method, nor was it allowed by the permits that had been issued to us by the Greek authorities. These surface scatters of sherds and other artifacts, which for convenience we call sites (see the definition above), do not always bear a close relationship to what might be buried underneath. It is a well known problem, and many an archaeologist has pondered it, dwelling on it optimistically or somberly, depending on whether he believed in surveys or not. Perhaps the most common objection is that on a long-inhabited site the earlier layers are covered by later ones, so that the investigator may fail to appreciate the earlier stages of its occupation and so runs the risk of underestimating its age. A surface site is the product of a host of natural and human factors, and in many cases we cannot truly say what might be underneath, a limitation we must keep firmly in mind when we ponder our results. Over and over again, however, archaeologists have found that nature, by eroding the edges of a site or through the burrowings of animals, or man, by plowing, has brought to the surface a surprisingly representative collection of what lies buried underneath. Of course, when a single period is represented by many large, fresh pieces of pottery and other artifacts, we have considerable confidence in the date. The determination of the function, date, and extent of a site can also sometimes be fairly firm, when architecture is present and visible at the surface.

Entire sites may have been buried so deeply that plows, foxes, or hedgehogs have failed to bring any evidence to the surface. How many such sites there might be in any given area obviously depends on how much territory has been covered deeply with sediment since the land became first occupied, something our geological survey was intended to ascertain. The sea also has to be held responsible for the concealment or destruction of sites. During the last glacial period, some 30,000 to 16,000 years ago, sea level was about 120 m lower than it is now, and the coastal plains that had emerged around the present land were certainly inhabited, if only sparsely. Since then the sea has steadily risen, flooding or washing away ancient sites and distorting the pattern of sites we look for, the more so the older the period of interest is. Even during the last few millennia this rise has continued, as it does today, and in the southern Argolid the Classical temples at Halieis and several Late Roman pottery kilns are now under 3 to 5 m of water. That many sites may thus have been lost to the sea caused us

concern and inspired a geophysical study offshore to establish the precise behavior of the migrating coastline. The results of the geological and geophysical studies have been quite comforting, and certainly on land we did not lose more than a tiny fraction of all sites due to burial. Though more sites may have existed offshore, it is fortunate that the sea drowned most of the land before the Argolid became densely inhabited and that its advance since the Bronze Age has not been large. Nevertheless, loss of coastal sites is something we must keep in mind.

The purpose of our fieldwork was to find sites, and about 320 of them were indeed found and duly recorded. This number includes the sites mapped in 1972, insofar as we have been able to verify their existence. For each site a form was filled out with a long list of its attributes, from the name of the present owner of the land to a description of its setting, adding a sketch map and other data useful for finding the spot again in the future and for interpreting its meaning once we should get around to examining our results. Sites were normally recognized from an abundance of artifacts, rendered obvious when the team members, calling out each one as soon as they saw it, joined in a rising chorus as the number of finds increased. To passing shepherds we must have presented a strange sight, this line of foreigners walking through the fields, shouting odd words over and over again.

If the team leader decided that a concentration of artifacts indeed warranted the designation of site, the area in question was immediately examined and recorded. The place in the traverse where the survey left off was marked with little flags; the site was put on the map, given a letter designating the area and a serial number (e.g., B100), and photographed. We then mapped each site simply by having the team members walk out slowly from another flag near the center until they reached the edge of the artifact scatter, which we usually defined as the place where the number of artifacts dropped to less than one per square meter. Next, the finds on the site were collected, to be brought back to the laboratory in Koiladha for identification. On sites too large for us to pick up all finds we randomly

chose a set of squares from which everything had to be gathered, to avoid bias due to a preference for one kind of object or another. If left to themselves some people might not pick up "dull" sherds; others would not look hard for items difficult to see, such as flint; and all were likely to avoid ground densely covered with thistles. Because of the perversity of nature, of course, quite often most or all of the best diagnostic material, such as coins or sherds of painted pottery, would lie between designated sampling squares. To get around that problem we walked each site once more to collect everything that seemed of interest, a grab bag that often contained by far the best material.

This procedure, so tedious to describe, served our purpose well because it was simple to carry out and took only about an hour for any but the largest sites. The mapping gave us an idea of the size of each site, and the samples usually sufficed to say when or how often it had been occupied, telling us commonly also something about what its function might have been. To clarify our own thinking on this last point, some of us one summer made an inventory of the durable artifacts around modern farmsteads in the area.

It is easy, as we have often done ourselves, to think of all sorts of pitfalls that might accompany this method. What is much less easy is to see how they can be avoided, short of excavating every site, which is patently impossible. What we tried to do was to gather as much data in as unbiased a way as

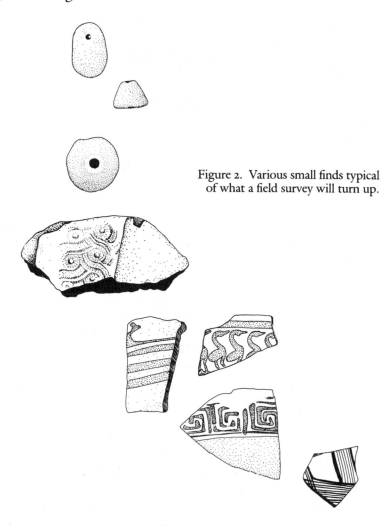

Figure 2. Various small finds typical of what a field survey will turn up.

possible with the time, money, and resources we had at our disposal, without skimming across the surface at such speed that we would miss important things. Until we are much more familiar with the natural and cultural processes that create surface sites from buried cultural remains, the method described here will have to suffice.

Once a site had been sampled, the team would collect its flags, resume walking, and start up its monotonous chant of "sherd . . . sherd." All the materials went back to our laboratory in an old school building in Koiladha, on the bay opposite Franchthi cave, where everything, no matter how insignificant it might seem, was saved in case other questions should arise later. The artifacts were washed, labeled, described, drawn or photographed if they warranted that, and packed. Today, the collection rests in the care of the Greek Archaeological Service, ready for future reference.

Almost our whole collection consists of objects made of stone or terra cotta. We found about 6,500 flaked tools of flint or obsidian (a black volcanic glass), as well as 200 or so millstones, hammers, and axes ground from other kinds of hard rock. Though lamps, figurines, spindle whorls, and other, more intriguing objects were indeed discovered, most of the 45,000 or so ceramic pieces are sherds of broken pots and roof tiles. A few objects of metal and glass, half a dozen coins of bronze or silver, a small number of bones and shells, and some odds and ends constitute the remainder of our discoveries, except for the architectural remains we left standing on the sites, where they are now falling victim to progress at a discouraging rate.

Caring for the collections was the job of each afternoon, done by the whole team under the supervision of specialists in various categories of finds. Rarely can so much time have been spent by so many on so visually unattractive a set of materials. Yet, together with the field maps, this work is the base on which rests the story we shall now begin to tell.

Chapter 3

•

Hunting the Wild Ass:
Earliest Man in
the Southern Argolid

During the first several million years of their existence human beings survived on what their skill and good fortune might extract from the offerings of nature. To Thomas Hobbes, in the middle of the seventeenth century, their lives seemed "solitary, poor, nasty, brutish, and short," but today we have a very different view. For a keen eye, for a hand equipped with a stone-tipped spear, or for a woman's gathering skills nature tends to be much more generous than we, in our managed and artificial world, can imagine. Even the few remaining hunters and gatherers, today surviving at the margins of deserts, do not have a particularly difficult time of it, except in rare periods of adversity. Neither did our Ice Age ancestors; and, few as they were in a large world and amidst a prolific nature, that is not surprising.

Icecaps, glaciers, and tundras full of woolly mammoths fill the image we have of the Ice Age. This sequence of 100,000 year long glacial periods separated by brief intervals of warmer interglacial climate began a few million years ago, and continues. We ourselves live near the end of an interglacial; it was shortly after its beginning that mankind, by domesticating plants and animals, finally began to overcome its dependence on the generosity of nature.

For the Mediterranean region, delicately perched between a northern belt of global westerly winds that generally bring rain, and a dry southern high-pressure zone, the conventional image of the Ice Age needs refurbishing. Here in the summer the subtropical condition prevails, sunny and dry, whereas in winter the westerly airflow across Europe moves southward to bring rain and cooler weather. With each glacial period, the southward advance of arctic conditions shifted the rain belt in the same direction, cooling the eastern Mediterranean by an average 2° to 5° C, and making it considerably drier, but mercifully sparing it burial by ice, merely bringing a few small mountain glaciers to Mount Olympus and other high ranges. Instead of the maquis and fir and pine forests that clothe the mountains today, glacial Greece appears to have been covered mainly with a sagebrush steppe, while a little woodland of pine and, in sheltered places, deciduous oak survived at intermediate levels. Dryness rather than the cold was probably the main reason for this drastically different landscape.

On present evidence, man's entry in the Greek peninsula came relatively late. A few controversial claims aside, the evidence, sparse as it is, indicates that they did not begin to explore the mountain ranges, steep valleys, and small plains of Greece until perhaps 200,000 years ago. Who the people were that, in small numbers, wandered through the empty spaces of this large, mountainous region we know only from the discovery of a single skull in a cave in Macedonia, a skull that evidently belonged to a primitive member of our own species. Nor are we much better informed about their mode of living, because all they left as a record of their passing are occasional stone tools in such uninformative places as river gravel bars or an ancient soil, where nothing remains to indicate the condition of their living. It is even later, in the Middle Palaeolithic, less than 100,000 years ago, that we find evidence of human beings settling in appreciable numbers in the western parts of Greece. They were probably Neanderthals, an early branch of *Homo sapiens*, recognized by their distinctive tools, which we find in caves and at open air sites in Epiros, Thessaly, and the Peloponnese.

The earliest evidence for a human presence in the southern Argolid consists of a small number of flaked flint tools of a type known as Mousterian, which we have found at four sites.

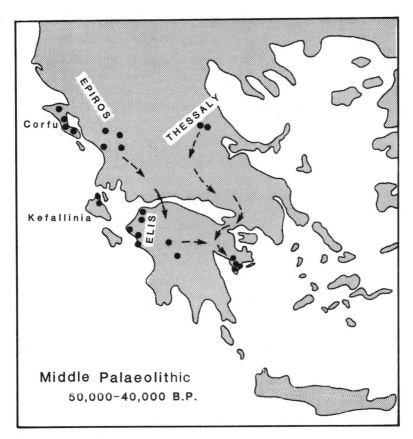

Map 5. The black dots on this map indicate the oldest confirmed traces of human presence in Greece. The arrows suggest how small bands of people, Neanderthalers, we presume, may have made their way south into the Peloponnese and to Franchthi cave. The two sites on the island of Kefallinia prove that even at this early date the open sea was no barrier to travel. If the coast seems distorted and unfamiliar, it is because the sea was then some 35 to 40 m lower than today, exposing a measure of coastal plain, and joining many islands to the mainland—for example, Corfu.

Radioactive isotopes contained in the thick calcareous crust in this semiarid climate, formed within ancient soils and on some artifacts buried in them, indicate that those people lived in or visited the area between 50,000 and 40,000 years ago.

That interval, nearly in the middle of the last glacial period, was relatively mild, but enough ice remained piled on northern

Figure 3. Middle Palaeolithic (Mousterian) stone tools and weapons from the southern Argolid.

lands to keep sea level down by approximately 40 m. As a result, a narrow coastal plain had emerged, which surrounded the entire Argolid and joined some of the islands to the mainland. In the southern Argolid, a steppe with scattered patches of trees covered the coastal plains, while open woods of pine and perhaps deciduous oak may have found a refuge in the shelter of the hills. Northern Greece, for which the evidence is better, had forests above the sagebrush-covered lowlands, where Middle Palaeolithic hunters went after mammoth, deer, antelope, ibex, aurochs (wild cattle), and even rhinoceros, as well as a species of now extinct European wild ass (*Equus hydruntinus*). What their quarry was in the Argolid we do not know.

The four or five Middle Palaeolithic sites of the southern Argolid are appropriately placed for hunters pursuing their quarry across the coastal plains and into the hills. One is in a gorge on a good route from the coastal plain at Ermioni to the well watered uplands around Iliokastro, where the discovery of a Mousterian flint flake by Jameson in 1958 indicated that Middle Palaeolithic hunters visited the plateau at the foot of Dhidhima mountain. The site is also near a deposit of brown flint, used until recently as material for stone tools. This statement may seem surprising, but stone tools—the material being free, and the tools easy to make—long remained a favorite in the Greek countryside for simple cutting and carving tasks or to light a fire. Today glass from Coca-Cola bottles occasionally serves the same purpose.

Another site, on the route between the bays of Franchthi and Ermioni, appears to have been used for toolmaking, leaving flint cores, flakes, debris, and a few tools for us to find. The source of this material is no longer visible, but the site was on the bank of a small stream, and cobbles of flint may have been

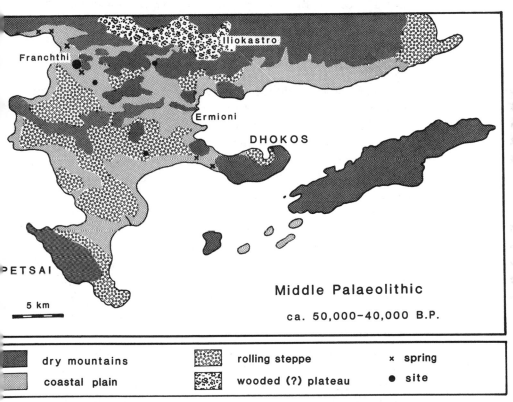

Map 6. In the southern Argolid we have found four small open air sites of Middle Palaeolithic age. Moreover, the Franchthi cave was also probably inhabited at this time. A coastal plain, watered here and there by copious springs that today flow beneath the sea, surrounded the peninsula and connected it with Dhokos and Spetsai islands. Large game, grazing in this plain, may have been the quarry of wandering hunters, who evidently also ventured inland, perhaps to take advantage of the deer, fruit, and acorns offered by pockets of oak woods in sheltered inland valleys.

used. A third site, represented by only a few stone points, was located favorably with respect to springs now below the sea, which provided a drinking place at the narrow neck of coastal plain that connected the mainland with what is today the island of Dhokhos.

Franchthi cave, where a thick sequence of deposits records human occupation from more than 25,000 years ago to the beginning of the Bronze Age, would have been a suitable base camp for Neanderthal hunters. Though its deepest strata have not been reached, we are told by the excavators that a few flint flakes of the right age have been found at the base of the excavation.

The Middle Palaeolithic interval, however, here lasting from 50,000 to 40,000 years ago or perhaps a little later, is long, and we cannot be certain that the sites assigned to this period were even contemporaneous. All were chance discoveries, and many others may have been destroyed by erosion or cultivation, or submerged by the sea. It is therefore premature to say much about Middle Palaeolithic living from such skimpy information.

Around 30,000 years ago, the climate began to deteriorate rather abruptly. Up to that time the landscape had been stable, with incised streams and little erosion, but now a colder and drier climate thinned out the protective plant cover, and even the diminished runoff was capable of laying down thick alluvial deposits, bright red in color, on valley floors and coastal plains. The world then entered a full glacial state, the coldest and presumably driest time of the entire last glacial period. Northern icecaps spread far south (though they did not come even close to Greece), drawing so much water from the oceans that the sea fell to about 120 m below its present level. This event exposed a broad coastal plain around the entire Argolid peninsula and connected Methana in the northeast with Attica, across what is now the Saronic Gulf.

As before we must infer the vegetation from what is known in northern Greece, where the palaeobotanical record, mainly based on fossil pollen taken from the mud of ancient lakes and peat bogs, is much better than in the waterless south. Up there, sagebrush steppe virtually eliminated the fir and pine forests, leaving mere remnants up in sheltered valleys where a little more rain or springwater was available. The southern Argolid must have been similarly dominated by steppe, as is confirmed by the kinds of seeds found in the deposits at Franchthi. These same deposits contain bones of the large herbivores one expects in such open country, mainly aurochs and the extinct

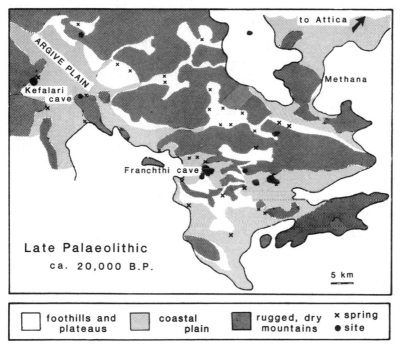

Map 7. At the height of the last glacial, between about 25,000 and 18,000 years ago, sea level was more than 100 m lower than today, and a vast coastal plain surrounded the mountainous heart of the Argolid. This plain was dry and steppe-like, covered mainly with sagebrush, but here and there near the present coast one can still find the campsites of Late Palaeolithic hunters, who went after the herds of wild cattle and ass that roamed the plain and gathered at the many now submarine springs. Late in summer, when the coast became too dry, small bands of people may have wandered up into the hills, where water, fruit, and game could be had even in the driest months of the year.

wild ass, and of small rodents typical for the steppe, whose tiny bones were perhaps left in the cave by birds of prey.

The turn to a very dry climate placed great value on perennial springs on the coastal plain, of which quite a few can still be found now spilling uselessly below the sea, near Franchthi cave, for example. These springs fed a vegetation more lush than elsewhere on the coastal plains, one that must have stayed green throughout the year, and they formed gathering points for the wandering herds of wild cattle and ass. Similar enclaves of richer growth and better hunting probably existed in some interior valleys and on upland plateaus such as that around Iliokastro. There, springs and streams still in evidence today may have created refuges wooded with pine and some deciduous oak, where deer might be taken in late summer and autumn.

Artifacts dating to the last glacial maximum are surprisingly scarce in the southern Argolid, more so even than those of the preceding Middle Palaeolithic. The excavation at Franchthi brought to light only a small number of stone tools of this Late Palaeolithic age, associated with animal bones and traces of fire, evidence for little more than the campsites of passing hunters. Nearby, on a hilltop opposite the cave with a commanding view of the coastal plain, some bladelets, evidently points for spears or arrows, and a few scrapers and other flint tools were found. One more point came from a rock shelter in the gorge halfway between Ermioni and the Iliokastro plateau. Even if these artifacts do not postdate the Late Palaeolithic, as well they might, they do not yield a pattern of exploitation of the area. Still, we cannot resist mentioning some possibilities.

The resources of the southern Argolid may have been slender during the glacial maximum, but they were not negligible. Rock- and mud-dwelling clams must have been present along the sandy and marshy coasts now deeply submerged below the sea, and small fish should have been easy to catch in its lagoons and from its beaches. The coastal plain, grassy and brushy, with incised streams, and probably mostly dry though locally watered by springs, provided wild ass, aurochs, and perhaps some red deer. In the spring there was an abundance of land snails, greens, tubers, and cereals. The stream banks, clad in shrubbery and small trees, would have furnished roots, bulbs, mushrooms, nuts and fruit, birds, and small animals; and the sheltered upland valleys, deer and hare, birds, fruit, and probably acorns. Obviously, dry and cold though the times may have been, this was not by any means a wasteland, but rather a set of resources easily as good as and probably better than what modern Bushmen make a reasonable living from in and around the Kalahari Desert. We tend to think of such hunters and gatherers as impoverished, eking out a precarious living always on the edge of starvation, but that misses the truth by a wide margin. The late glacial and postglacial environments of Europe, even those of the dry Mediterranean, were far richer than the Australian and African deserts where most modern hunter-gatherers live. Yet even those, the last carriers of a once great human tradition, tend to live well enough. An anthropologist who spent much time with them described with some amusement the leisurely awakening of the band, the relaxed breakfast, and the ensuing discussion of what they should have for dinner. Decision made, appropriate members march off to known places to acquire the necessities; the rest remain in camp to talk or sleep the day away. Estimates agree that as few as two or three hours per day are all such people normally must spend on providing the daily food. Not surprisingly, the end of the era of hunting and gathering has sometimes been called the true end of human affluence.

The resources listed above are plausible for conditions in the Argolid during the glacial period, but we have little evidence that they were actually exploited by Late Palaeolithic man. Of course, the Franchthi cave was 6 km from the sea at that time, and if fish and shellfish had been extensively consumed, one would expect the residue to have been left by the seashore rather than carried back to the cave. Some small mounds that may be ancient shell middens indeed exist at a 13,000 year old shore, now deeply submerged. It is therefore no surprise that remains of seafood have not been found in the cave. The palaeobotanical record at Franchthi, the remains of seeds, twigs, or leaves in the cave deposits, is poor and rather inconclusive. Bone finds, on the other hand, testify to the hunting of wild ass, red deer, and some wild cattle.

Reviewing once more what the environment probably was like, we realize that the coastal plains were most productive from late winter to early summer, whereas during the dry months of late summer and autumn the uplands would have provided better hunting and a more reliable supply of water. Thus seasonal migration between the coast and inland valleys or plateaus might have been a sensible practice. Sites such as Franchthi or the Kefalari cave, in the Argive plain, would have been suitable lowland camps, and the site above Ermioni or the caves in a gorge at Kleisoura, north of the Argive plain, might have served as way stations. Of the required upland camps, however, we have not a trace in our area; they may not have been in the southern Argolid in any case.

On the other hand, the wanderings on the coastal plain of red deer and wild ass and cattle need not have included the interior at all; dispersal during the wet season and congregation in the dry months near major springs would constitute an alternative mode of behavior. If that were the case, sites like Franchthi, or like Kefalari with its rich remains of highly successful Late Palaeolithic hunts, were perhaps year-round base camps, with hunting camps elsewhere, in caves or in the open air wherever sparse remains of the period have by chance been found.

Regrettably, the first proposition cannot be proved even for Epiros, in northern Greece, for which it was first formulated by the late Eric S. Higgs; and neither of the two can be tested with the sparse data from the southern Argolid. In fact, even the artifacts at Franchthi may represent no more than sporadic excursions by small bands into the periphery of some heartland elsewhere, the remains of temporary hunting camps, none permanent, and perhaps none tied to a regular pattern of ex-

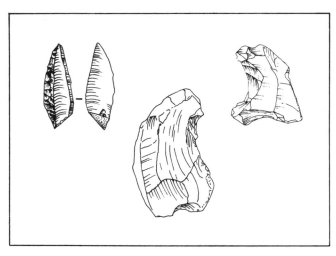

Figure 4. Stone tools and weapons of the Late Palaeolithic hunters in the southern Argolid.

ploitation. The issue remains open; the thin scatter of Late Palaeolithic sites across Greece, even thinner than that of the Middle Palaeolithic, does not help us to understand how the Ice Age inhabitants of Greece made their living, because it is so clearly in the main a product of the accidents of a desperately insufficient search and discovery.

Many millennia of very cold weather later the climate took, after a slow start, a definitive turn for the better. It became warmer, and, more important, the rainfall increased considerably. In northern and central Greece pine woods spread in the mountains, and oak forests expanded at lower elevations. Also the sea began to rise rapidly about 13,000 years ago. At Franchthi, bones of wild cattle are abundant among the animal remains left over from this time, and the first appearance of pistachio nuts, almonds, and other plants of a richer vegetation about 11,000 years ago heralded the arrival of a milder, more moist climate. Soon afterward, between 8,000 and 7,000 years ago, the climate reached its postglacial optimum. Evidence from North Africa and the Near and Middle East suggests that it may even have been a little wetter than it is now, with more summer rains, owing to a northward extension of the East African monsoons.

Mostly by inference from pollen records in northern and central Greece, with a dose of common sense reasoning, we assume (though some others think otherwise) that during the climate optimum the Argolid was largely covered with a deciduous oak woodland, with some beech, holly, and hornbeam, growing best on the deep soils of the southern hills, the wider valley bottoms, and the well watered upland plateaus. These woods would probably have been fairly open, more like parkland perhaps, and may have carried an understory of what are today the main shrubs of the maquis, such as evergreen oak, juniper, and pistachio. Dense shrubbery with many useful plants, such as wild cherry and plum, wild grape, pear, and almond, probably fringed the incised streams.

These environmental changes are confirmed by what has been found in the latest Palaeolithic and early Mesolithic deposits of Franchthi cave. Wild ass and ibex, still hunted during latest Palaeolithic time, vanished with the beginning of the Mesolithic, about 10,000 years ago. The aurochs, fond of the grasslands of the moister early postglacial, first increased, then disappeared when the woodland became too dense and dry for its taste, and wild boar and especially the large red deer took over. Fruit and nuts, peas, lentils, vetch, oats, and barley, all still wild, appear among the debris left by the Mesolithic dwellers of the cave. Land snails were also used, at times in large quantities.

During the melting of the icecaps the sea rose rapidly, but around 8,000 years ago most of the ice was gone, and the rise, having reached about 25 m below the present level, began to slow, continuing at a gentler pace to the present day. During the fast part of the rise the shore moved rapidly landward and was therefore generally either rocky or endowed with thin beaches of gravel and cobbles, the habitat of a limited suite of rock-dwelling mollusks. Only when the rise slowed down did the embayments of the Argolid coast acquire the sandy beaches, marshes, mud shoals, and inlets that are still there today. Along those shores, then as now, many different kinds of shellfish and fish could be found, as well as greens valued for the table, and rushes and reeds for many uses. Remains of most of these one finds preserved in the deposits laid down in Franchthi cave at this time.

Beginning with the latest Palaeolithic, around 11,000 years ago, one can see the approach of the shore and its changing environments reflected in the presence and kinds of shells and fishbones in the deposits of Franchthi cave. First come the limpets and marine snails typical for rocky shores, probably the only ones that could be found along the cliffs and cobble beaches of the rapidly rising sea. Somewhat later, about 9,000 B.P. (before the present), however, new species appear in the cave that are typical of the sand beaches, marshes, and mud shoals that began to form nearby at this time.

The milder climate and lusher vegetation greatly increased the range and abundance of resources over those of glacial times. The Mediterranean deciduous oak forest, even in its drier aspects, is quite rich. Together with the valley floors and the coastal plains it offered a varied harvest of greens, root crops, and bulbs in spring and early summer, fruit and nuts in summer and fall. Wild oats and barley could be harvested on more open, sunny slopes. All this supported red deer and wild boar and smaller game such as hares. In addition, the people of the earlier Mesolithic certainly would not have shunned, if need be, the meat of birds, lizards, or small rodents.

As before, the better watered uplands probably were the most productive. Especially in the dry late summer and early fall they must have stood out for their game and for a generous harvest of acorns (one notes that until very recently, acorns of the valonia oak, a very edible kind, were exported from the region for various purposes). On the other hand, the richness and variety of the postglacial uplands were offset to some degree by the loss of coastal land caused by the rising sea. By 10,000 years ago, those plains had shrunk from about 40 percent of the total area of the southern Argolid to less than 20 percent. Since then they have been reduced once again by half during the continued slow rise of the sea. With those plains vanished the wild ass, and a little later the wild cattle.

When we compare the list of resources available during the glacial maximum with those of early postglacial time, it is easy to see that the dramatic changes in their abundance, kinds, and distribution must have had a large impact on the mode of living of the Late Palaeolithic and Mesolithic inhabitants of the area, and everywhere else in Europe, too, for that matter. It is one thing to trail herds of large grazing animals on an open plain, and quite another to make a living by hunting deer in forests, catching fish along the shore, and gathering acorns, wild cereals, and fruit in the valleys. It is this drastic change in environmental opportunities that gave a very different cast to life, compared with what it was like during the full glacial.

In Greece, Mesolithic sites are even more rare than those of the Palaeolithic, so rare in fact that the only sensible conclusion is that we have so far failed to find even a small fraction of those that must once have been there. The only one confirmed outside the southern Argolid is on the island of Corfu, in the extreme northwest, where a midden of shells and other kitchen refuse dating to the latest Mesolithic has been excavated. In the southern Argolid, Franchthi cave is the only site, although some flint flakes found in a cave in the upper Fournoi valley may also be of Mesolithic age. At Franchthi, the thick deposits and rich variety of artifacts and residue make it clear that this was a major site, semipermanently or permanently occupied since the very latest Palaeolithic.

Might Franchthi cave have been a base camp, key to a seasonal mode of existence, on the coast from midwinter through summer, and in the uplands in late summer and autumn? That would be in accord with the botanical finds, which indicate a long occupation in summer and spring. On the other hand, our lack of success, notwithstanding a diligent search, in finding other sites that would fit a pattern of seasonal exploitation speaks against this possibility.

Alternatively, the area might have been exploited exclusively from the Franchthi base, in accord with evidence from the seasonal growthlines of shells, suggesting that, at least by the end

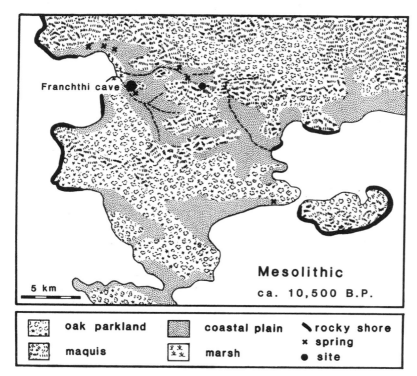

Map 8. The milder climate returning after the glacial period converted the southern Argolid into an open oak parkland, with maquis on the stony flanks of the mountains. The sea had risen considerably since the continental icecaps had begun to melt, wiping out much of the coastal plain and with it the herds of wild cattle and ass. The better climate, however, perhaps even a little wetter than it is today, provided other game in the woods and on the upland plateaus, while sandy and marshy shores invited fishing and the collecting of shellfish. Nevertheless, the area remained very thinly settled; we are certain only of the Franchthi site at this time. Dashed lines indicate the principal streams, probably mostly dry in summer.

of the Mesolithic, the inhabitants collected their shellfish throughout the year rather than in any single season. That would, however, exclude a thorough exploitation of the whole southern peninsula, because the distances are too great to do so without overnight camps, and we find no evidence for those even in obvious spots such as the Iliokastro plateau or the narrows on the coastal plain near Dhokhos island. Such sites may, of course, have existed, but they cannot have been numerous.

All this evidence for an unexploited potential is a bit mysterious, given the propensity of human beings to multiply to the
limits of nature's resource potential. The millennia that elapsed
between the first persistent occupation at Franchthi and the arrival of the Neolithic agricultural age, 8,000 years ago, were
certainly time enough to achieve more than just a single site
accommodating probably no more than 25 to 50 people.

Clearly, we find ourselves encouraged to think of explanations other than the simple convenience of a small band in
finding enough to eat for the selection of Franchthi as a permanent occupation site, for the apparent lack of full exploitation
of the area, and for the absence of significant growth over
so long a time. Some scattered pieces of evidence indeed point
in the direction of other, more controversial but intriguing
possibilities.

Obsidian, a black volcanic glass, has excellent qualities for
the making of durable, sharp tools, so excellent, in fact, that
even an occasional modern surgeon has found it to his taste. It
is not a common rock, and in the Aegean the number of potential sources is small. Each of those has a characteristic chemical
signature that allows us to say with certainty from which volcano a given supply has been taken. Obsidian was known at
Franchthi around 11,000 years ago, during the latest Palaeolithic. It came, as it has come ever since, from Melos, one of
the many small islands in the southern Aegean, an island that
was, like most of the others in the Cycladic archipelago, not
settled until the Bronze Age.

The source on Melos is not obvious to the seafarer passing
offshore, and its discovery, certainly by chance, implies that as
early as 11,000 or 12,000 years ago the islands of the Aegean
had been explored fairly thoroughly, though probably only occasionally. In fact, the discovery might have come even earlier,
during the height of the last glacial, when sea level was so low
that many of the islands had merged into a single Cycladic
landmass. Melos was then but a few kilometers offshore, an
easy trip when taking advantage of the daily land and sea
breezes. Boats or rafts must have been available, for seafaring

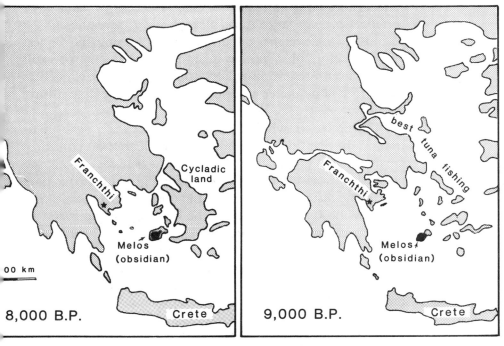

Map 9. Obsidian, a black volcanic glass, was much sought after in pre-historic Greece because it makes such fine cutting tools. Appearing at Franchthi as early as 11,000 years ago, it came from Melos, but we do not know when it was first discovered on this one small island among the many that dot the Aegean Sea. Palaeolithic hunters may have come upon it during the last glacial maximum, when the sea was low and the island easily reached, but we have no evidence that they did so. Later, Melos had to be reached by boat; perhaps fishermen returning from the rich fishing grounds of the central Aegean picked up a few pieces on their way home. The coastlines of these maps are as they were at the times represented.

skills were not foreign even to Palaeolithic man. The island of Kefallinia, for example, then as now separated from the west coast of Greece by the sea, had already been settled in the Middle Palaeolithic. Lest this seem implausible, we note that about 40,000 years ago human beings crossed very much wider waters, so wide that land could not have been seen on the other side, to settle Australia from Indonesia.

Around 8,000 years ago, the abundance of obsidian increased noticeably at Franchthi, and at about the same time vertebrae of very large tuna, perhaps up to several hundred pounds in live weight, became common among the bones. Whereas before only modest quantities of the bones of small fish had been present, now large tuna constituted as much as half of the bone material, testifying to a considerable fishing activity.

On steep coasts, where cold, nutrient-rich water wells up to fertilize the sea, tuna sometimes come close to shore, but they are not readily caught from the beach. As best we can tell, the most fertile seas and thus the best fishing grounds at this time were some distance away, along the northeastern coast of the Akte, in the Cyclades, and on the east side of the island of Euboea, in the northern Aegean. This leads us to suggest that the inhabitants of Franchthi cave compensated for the disappearance of large game from the shrinking coastal plain after the ninth millennium B.P. by fishing rather than by exploiting the resources of upland plateaus and valleys. Having already been aware for some time of the value of Melian obsidian, the Franchthiotes may from time to time have used their extended fishing voyages to acquire small amounts from others, who had obtained it directly on Melos and knew the way. Perhaps the inhabitants of the cave might even have found themselves induced to go there on their own account to procure more of this valuable and useful material.

At the same time that obsidian became more available and big fish became a diet staple, the dwellers in the cave suddenly chose to be very selective in their use of shellfish. Previously, during the latest Palaeolithic, they had gathered whatever was obtainable on the rocky and cobbly shores, but just when the choice became much larger because many new edible species of beach, mud flat, and shoal had appeared, the Franchthiotes chose to concentrate mainly on only one, collecting huge numbers of a tiny, buttonlike snail called *Cyclope neritea*, an inhabitant of open marshy shores. It is a curious choice, because the animal is rather too small to make a decent meal, a snack at best. In fact, the vast majority of the shells found in the cave had been perforated, probably to allow them to be strung into necklaces or other jewelry. The only other marine mollusk found fairly frequently in the Mesolithic cave deposits is a rather larger snail living in a much wider range of environments, *Cerithium vulgare*. It can be eaten, certainly, but, combined with *Cyclope*, it represents a peculiar selection from the rather large array of edible marine mollusks available in the neighborhood of the cave. Today *Cerithium* is sometimes used as bait for fishing, and it is tempting to think that Mesolithic fishermen used it for the same purpose, shunning cockles and other clams in favor of a dish of tuna.

Why this emphasis on *Cyclope*, and why was obsidian, a good cutting material but not indispensable, needed so badly that it was worth trading or even traveling for? We do not know, and it is perhaps reckless to suggest on such slim evidence that Franchthi was on the way toward becoming some sort of regional trade center. Nevertheless, we are tempted to think that this was the first glimmer of a new economy, no longer exclusively dependent on extracting the community's needs from the local environment, but instead looking outward to a greater region for its survival—and for something more. The geographic position of Franchthi, not particularly logical for the mere purpose of local subsistence, would have been a favorable one if a network of outside contacts had begun to acquire equal importance with local food supplies.

Chapter 4

.

An Outpost of the
Agricultural Revolution

While the Franchthiotes were still hunting wild asses in the steppe, at best worrying a little about the shrinking coastal plains and what they might do for a living in the future, the Near and Middle East were in the first throes of what would prove to be the most momentous change ever in human life and society. There, some 11,000 years ago, a few people shifted from a complete dependence on, or at most a limited degree of management of, the bounty of nature to an ever increasing measure of direct control over their production of food. The transition, no doubt, was almost imperceptible; from hunting wild sheep to the careful culling of the superfluous males and the weak from the flock is but a small step. No larger is the change from harvesting wild grain to keeping out the competing weeds, to collecting seed and sowing it, accidentally at first maybe, at another, more convenient or better-watered spot. Many have been the speculations on what brought about this agricultural revolution, a climate change, perhaps, that reduced nature's potential, or a population explosion increasing the need for food beyond what the environment, left to itself, could provide. Maybe people grew extra grain or raised sheep for wool to trade for flint or wives with neighbors living in the next valley over the ridge. Perhaps the whole thing was no more than an accident or the result of the typical human love for experimentation. In any case, with this new way of sustaining life came freedom from many constraints, even today not so much as we should like to think, but enough to alter fundamentally the structure and quality of human life and its relation to nature. Whether a population increase came first or afterward, it was agriculture that made it possible to feed many more people than hunting and gathering could have. Agricultural production, farming, made it possible to produce much more food from a given area of land than hunting or gathering, and eventually specialized skills, professions such as that of village potter, became both possible and necessary, as the people came to live near their fields and to store their seasonal bounty. Incidentally, it also somehow removed the restrictions on the birthrate that keep hunter-gatherers from exceeding the limits of their resources. It was the agricultural revolution that made it possible for a few to feed many, that required a settled life, and that led to a differentiation of society into farmers, craftsmen, traders, soldiers, priests, and rulers. It was the agricultural revolution also that, partly because of the need for leadership and organization, for example, to build and manage irrigation works, and partly because of a peculiar human genius for bureaucracy, brought us as early as 5,000 years ago the organized state and its inevitable companions: offices, officials, and officiousness.

Wavelike, the agrarian mode spread outward from its eastern origins, reaching the Greek shores of the Aegean about 8,000 years ago. Whether it was carried physically by immigrants with their seeds and flocks, was transmitted by some combination of word of mouth, example, and exchange from one group to the next, or arose, in part, locally and independently, the wave rolled swiftly on to central Europe in the fifth millennium B.C. and to the shores of the Atlantic Ocean in the fourth.

The early agricultural period in the southern Argolid, the Neolithic, spanned 3,000 years, from 6000 to just before 3000 B.C. Elsewhere, in the Middle East and Anatolia, for example, or in northern Greece, this was a time of great social and economic change, but in the Argolid the changes appear to have been less drastic, and the landscape remained largely unaltered through those many years. The fauna reflected in the animal bones of the Franchthi deposits suggests that a slightly drier climate may have opened up the woodlands somewhat, but the plant remains do not imply any great difference, and even as late as the Early Bronze Age some rich oak woods remained in the area. The coastal zone, though continuing its slow march inland, retained much the same environments that had existed during the Mesolithic.

Though one awaits further analysis of the Franchthi data, the only truly novel elements in the older Neolithic strata of the cave seem to be the bones of domesticated sheep and goats; at the same time the first domesticated lentils and early species of domesticated grains appear. Otherwise, the record suggests that life entered the new agrarian era without a marked break. Pottery may not have arrived on the scene until a little later, and the preferential gathering of the snail *Cerithium vulgare* continued for some time before it was replaced by a less eclectic and more obviously useful assemblage of cockles and other edible clams available at the adjacent shore.

During most of the long Neolithic period the southern Argolid was very thinly settled. Even our intensive survey has failed to find a second Early Neolithic site, and only a few others, small ones, are known for the Middle and Late Neolithic. Accordingly, the influence of the Neolithic inhabitants of Franchthi on the surrounding landscape, farmers and herders though they must have been, was surely small. Little land needed to be cleared for agriculture, and we should not expect, nor do we see, any evidence of soil erosion. On the other hand, extensive grazing over thousands of years tends to degrade woodland, as the palaeobotanical record of the cave seems to confirm, suggesting a first step toward the eventual replacement of the oak woods with today's maquis.

The Early Neolithic at Franchthi displayed an agricultural economy based on the cultivation of wheat, barley, and lentils, combined with the herding of sheep and goats, fishing, and some shellfish gathering. A little later, other changes began to distinguish these first farmers from their Mesolithic predecessors or, perhaps, ancestors. Dry stone walls were built on the shore in front of the cave at the beginning of the sixth millennium B.C. At about the same time or soon afterward, mill-stones made of various materials appeared, as well as a few imported axes or hoes of ground stone and a technology for making flaked stone tools that relied much on Melian obsidian. In addition, one finds unpainted ceramics, ornaments cut from stone and shell, and a few human figurines made of clay. The evidence in general favors a replacement of the indigenous Mesolithic population by Neolithic settlers following a broadly Near Eastern pattern, although some elements of their culture suggest a more gradual, less intrusive development of new practices.

Curiously, Franchthi has a Neolithic occupation as old as any in Greece. It is also thus far the only place where occupation was continuous from the latest Palaeolithic on. If some or all of the Neolithic inhabitants of Franchthi cave indeed came from abroad, where might their homeland have been? Elsewhere in Greece, in Thrace, Macedonia, Thessaly, and even on Crete, extensive colonization of the hitherto virtually empty land is evident, and the close similarity of those early villages there to contemporary ones in Anatolia suggests immigration from the east by land or by sea. Those who introduced the new practices at Franchthi may have come directly across the sea or by way of the more densely settled north, but their property and way of life were so similar to those of people living at the same time from Pakistan to the Balkans that we may never be able to trace their origin.

Even so, the Neolithic settlers of Greece did not all behave in the same manner, nor did they all show a preference for similar sites. In the north they favored the low ground of inland basins and river valleys and their adjacent foothills and, once established, spread across the land in an orderly way until all open spaces were filled with a dense pattern of small villages, today marked by distinctive artificial mounds. In the process, the primordial oak woods disappeared from Thessaly, Boeotia, and parts of Macedonia and Thrace. In the Peloponnese, on the other hand, settlements were few and far from each other. The early settlers there seem to have favored coastal

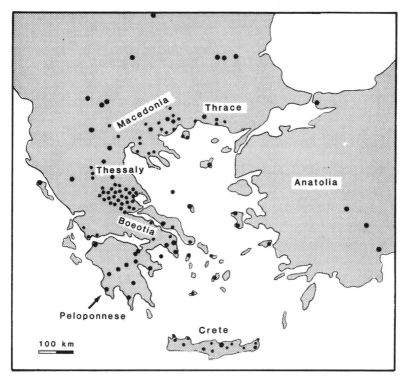

Map 10. Very early in the Neolithic, people who practiced farming and the herding of sheep and goats came out of Anatolia to Greece. In the course of a few thousand years they thickly settled the fertile river plains of Thrace, Macedonia, and Thessaly, where mounds concealing the remains of their villages still dot the landscape. The sea was apparently no barrier to them, because they colonized Crete early, but they did not favor the Cycladic islands or the Peloponnese, where their settlements were few and far apart. Black dots mark the most important of the many Neolithic sites, and the coastline is shown as it was 6,000 years ago.

rather than inland locations, and more often than not they failed to spread out to fill the space available like their contemporaries did in the north.

These differences between north and south are intriguing, as is too the question why Neolithic settlers came to the Peloponnese at all so early on, when richer, better-watered lands were still available in abundance farther north. Early Neolithic

Greece certainly was not yet so densely populated that there existed anywhere a serious competition for arable or grazing land. What, then, was the incentive for people who had been sedentary in their homeland to pack up their families, property, and livestock, and travel to places as difficult of access as Crete or as unpromising as Franchthi? Having done so, why did they select places to settle so strikingly different from those preferred by their fellow immigrants in Thessaly and farther north?

Since the answers are far from clear, a little speculation can be forgiven us in regard to so fascinating a set of questions. Many of the Neolithic sites of the Peloponnese have much in common. They are often on the coast, in or near a cave, and near copious springs that watered small coastal meadows, as some of them still do. What Franchthi, the best known example, had to offer was more than a fine natural shelter, several springs, and a modestly productive countryside. There was also its location between the more numerous settlements of the Argive plain and the Cycladic islands, including Melos of the excellent obsidian, a location that, as we noted in the previous chapter, may have had considerable advantage. On the other hand, good soils were comparatively scarce, and the permanent rivers and more dependable rainfall of northern Greece were absent.

Where did Franchthi's farmers farm? The streams had cut their channels deep in the valleys since the last glacial period and, flowing rarely and only in the winter, seldom if ever flooded their banks. Farming the small river plains, and even more the southern hills (where the soils were good), therefore meant putting one's hopes on rain, but rain-fed agriculture is an uncertain proposition in the dry and variable Argolid climate. The best soils, whether in the valleys or on the hills, required the clearing of woodland, and quite a lot of it, too, because excess harvests are a necessity when next year's rain cannot be depended on. Below the cave, however, the Franchthiotes had available a more dependable place to grow crops, where many springs, then above the sea, watered small meadows. Similar spring-fed meadows still exist here and there along the shores of the Peloponnese, where they carry a lush vegetation, green throughout the summer. The practice of growing crops on spring meadows goes back a long way, having been tried first, so far as we know, by the earliest settlers at Jericho, about 10,000 years ago. Such wetlands provide a yield that can be depended upon from year to year and with very little risk. Though we cannot prove that the people at Franchthi farmed in this manner, it is suggestive that, at the same time as domesticated grains appear in the cave deposits, the wild ones vanish, an unlikely event if the newly cultivated fields had been on the same slopes and valley bottoms where wild cereals were common weeds.

The land, in all likelihood, was worked with hoes and digging sticks, probably fitted with the small Neolithic stone axes, rather than plowed. These little axes would have been useless for clearing woodland, and without a plow it would have been exceedingly hard work to turn the soil deeply enough to permit the rain to water a crop of wheat or barley. Evidence for ards (scratch plows) and draft animals, however, does not appear anywhere until the Bronze Age. Reliance on spring fed agriculture would make clearing and plowing unnecessary, but it would obviously have limited the number of inhabitants, because spring meadows were neither common nor extensive. The food supply might have been augmented by herding flocks of sheep and goats on the maquis-covered slopes and, together with pigs, in the open oak woods, a practice that leaves few traces for the archaeologist. Even so, the growth of the population would have been severely and permanently restricted, as indeed seems to have been the case in the southern Argolid for almost 3,000 years. Moreover, spring meadows are scarce elsewhere in the Peloponnese also, and if they were a condition for Neolithic survival in that southern climate and on those southern soils, it is not surprising that the number of Neolithic sites there remained small. Still, we find it difficult to imagine that it took 3,000 years to invent or import the simple scratch plows that finally permitted the use of so much more land in the final

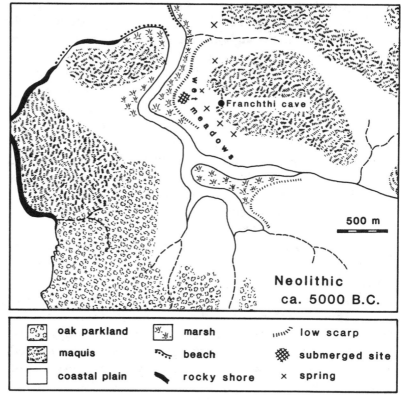

Neolithic ca. 5000 B.C.

oak parkland	marsh	low scarp
maquis	beach	submerged site
coastal plain	rocky shore	× spring

Map 11. During the Neolithic, with the sea still somewhat farther away than it is now, the Franchthi cave overlooked·a narrow inlet bordered by marshes, where today one finds Koiladha bay. Several streams, probably dry for most of the year, shown here with dashed lines, entered the inlet. The cave itself was inhabited, and stone structures were built on the slope outside. Archaeological materials, probably part of the same settlement, have also been found a few hundred meters offshore, now under more than 4 m of mud and 5 m of water. The inhabitants of Franchthi village probably farmed the spring-fed meadows on the terrace above the inlet, grazed their sheep and goats on the coastal plain and in the hills, and manufactured shell beads in front of the cave. They also gathered whatever fruit, nuts, and greens the surrounding countryside offered, and hunted and fished to supplement their diet.

Neolithic and Early Bronze Age. Nor do we take seriously the possibility that the Neolithic Peloponnesians were a curmudgeonly lot who would sooner not have lived within sight of the smoke of their neighbors' fires, like some of the crustier American settlers of the eighteenth and nineteenth centuries. Why then would anyone have tried to settle the Peloponnese at all?

Perhaps the reasons were different from the traditionally assumed search for land that would permit subsistence agriculture, the search for a place where all one's material needs could be satisfied by the products of the adjacent soil, augmented by a bit of herding, hunting, fishing, and gathering. Although the Franchthiotes evidently depended on the traditional Mediterranean practices of growing grains and herding sheep and goats, the fact that they never exploited the full potential of their surroundings suggests that something more than mere survival was involved.

For this additional element we look toward the geographic situation of Franchthi cave or, for that matter, of many of the other Neolithic sites in the Peloponnese, which are well placed to maintain trade contacts throughout the southern Aegean and across the Peloponnese. A large assortment of raw materials and finished products has been found at Franchthi that points to a pattern of regional exchange. Obsidian, honey-colored flint, marble, the volcanic rock andesite, superbly suited for millstones, and even semiprecious stones such as cornelian were brought to Franchthi from places sometimes hundreds of kilometers away. The imports take the form of vessels, ornaments, beads, cores and blades for toolmaking, and other artifacts. In exchange, salt might have been extracted locally from lagoons like those at Thermisi and Ververonda, which have been used more recently for the same purpose. There was also a small industry at the site, making beads from common cockleshells, though possibly merely for local use. Perhaps also some of the spectacular bracelets carved from the heavy shells of the spiny oyster *Spondylus gaederopus*, which were widely traded across southeastern and central Europe during the Neolithic, may have been manufactured there.

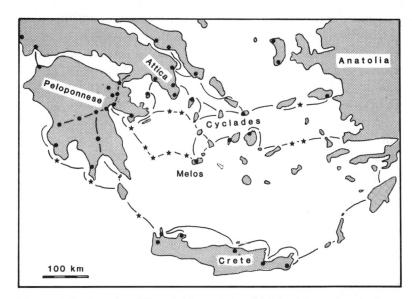

Map 12. The deposits of Franchthi cave have yielded evidence that the inhabitants gathered raw materials and finished products from many parts of the Aegean. This meant travel by boat, but the boats of the time did not cover more than 30 to 50 km per day, and had to be drawn up at night on a beach, where fresh water and shelter against pilferers were available. Small uninhabited islands would have been particularly favored, and, sea level still being some 10 to 15 m lower than now, many islets that are today mere rocks in the sea (stars) would have served well as stopover points. Together with many as yet uninhabited small Cycladic islands, these stepping stones formed a convenient network of trade routes between east and west, south and north. The village at Franchthi was favorably located on routes between Melos and the southern Cyclades and between Attica and the Peloponnese. Coasts and islands are shown as they appeared about 6,000 years ago. Black dots mark the principal Neolithic sites of the region.

It is possible that Franchthi was occupied throughout the year in the Early and Middle Neolithic, as would be expected if the livelihood of the inhabitants were based on spring-fed agriculture, herding, and trade, and if this last activity had been a reason for the selection of the site. The trade itself might have occurred while the Franchthiotes moved their flocks over long distances from summer to winter pastures. More likely, it might have taken place by sea, an elaboration of the tradition we proposed earlier for the later Mesolithic, of bringing chunks of obsidian home from distant tuna fishing voyages.

The Franchthi settlement existed in isolation for more than a thousand years, and only a few small additional sites appeared during the Middle and Late Neolithic. Traces of Middle Neolithic occupation occur in two caves, both well placed to be shepherd's camps; one of them, north of Dhidhima, is still so used today. Another cave site, probably serving the same purpose, was added in the Late Neolithic. We do not regard

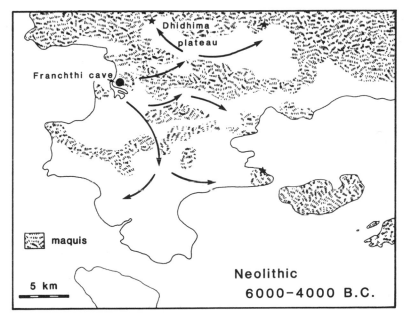

Map 13. During the Neolithic neither the number of sites nor the number of people in the southern Argolid increased much, and for more than 2,000 years Franchthi village remained the only sizable settlement. After about a thousand years, a few other sites (stars) appeared, all small. They are found in caves near grazing land, mainly the maquis, and were only occupied during the fifth millennium B.C. Probably shepherds' huts or sheepfolds, they may indicate an increase in the importance of sheep and goats, and thus of wool. The arrows on this map trace the most convenient paths from Franchthi through valleys and gorges to outlying pastures along the coast or on upland plateaus. The coast appears as it was about 6,000 years ago.

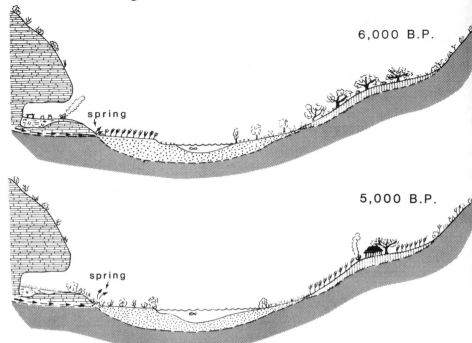

Figure 5. For a long time, the small tracts of wet meadowland at Franchthi, together with herding, some hunting and fishing, and perhaps a little trade, appear to have sufficed to feed the Neolithic population there. This, of course, limited the size of the population. One assumes that local Neolithic technology was not yet up to the task of clearing and cultivating the coastal plain or the oak parkland on the hills across the bay. To raise a crop of wheat or barley there, with only the winter rains to water it, would have required plows and draft animals. During the fourth millennium B.C., however, this problem must have been solved, because the cave was deserted, and several small settlements sprang up near the deep, fertile soils on the hills across the bay. The cave is in limestone resting on impermeable bedrock (dark tone) elsewhere covered with slope mantle (vertical shading) or valley fill (dotted pattern).

even this modest increase in the number of sites as evidence for an expanding population—indeed, even Franchthi may not have been continuously occupied during this period—but we see it rather as a shift in the mode of exploitation toward more pastoralism, perhaps because wool could be used to greater advantage. An abundance of loom weights and spindle whorls in the Franchthi deposits confirms that the production of cloth was important there during the fifth and fourth millennia B.C., as seems to have been the case elsewhere in Greece also.

It was only in the final half of the fourth millennium B.C. that this static scene began to change with the appearance of several new sites. These are open air settlements where finds of abundant pottery, millstones, axes, and the stone blades of sickles, polished from the cutting of cereals or grass, suggest that they were continuously inhabited places, not just sheepfolds. Their location clearly indicates the opening up of farmland in places never cultivated before, and thereby of a new era in the southern Argolid.

Chapter 5
•
Civilization Coming

Some years ago, Colin Renfrew, now Professor of Archaeology and Anthropology at Cambridge University, wrote an influential book on the origins of the Bronze Age in the Aegean and called it *The Emergence of Civilization*. A rather grand title, perhaps, but proper if a sudden spread of settlements with diverse functions, the simultaneous disappearance of the pristine landscape, and a striking increase in the variety of tools, art objects, and buildings constitute evidence of civilization. Fair enough; there is certainly no better point in the history of the southern Argolid to introduce this term than the moment the land began to be broadly settled. Moreover, although the surveying archaeologist is seldom enchanted by the beauty of the objects exposed at the surface, it is with the beginning of the Bronze Age that the civilized pleasure of finding objects of some beauty was afforded us occasionally. At this same point we begin to have far more knowledge; where in previous chapters we always could, and sometimes had to, bring in every available detail, from now on we must pick and choose and paint with a broader brush.

The term Bronze Age is to some extent a misnomer. Artifacts made of copper appear long before the official start of the Bronze Age, 5,000 years ago, though not in the southern Argolid. Nor is it so that Bronze Age sites and Bronze Age cultures can be invariably identified by their content of bronze tools, weapons, or ornaments. Far from it; for a long time the metal was actually rather scarce and evidently reserved for spe-

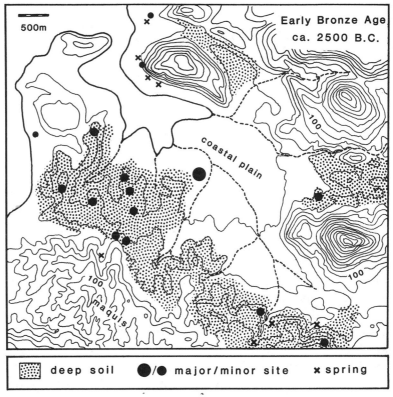

500m

Early Bronze Age
ca. 2500 B.C.

coastal plain

100

100

100

maquis

☒ deep soil   ●/● major/minor site   ✗ spring

Map 14. For more than 20,000 years Franchthi had been the human focus of the southern Argolid, but in the fourth millennium B.C. settlements began to spread across the landscape. Many small sites, probably farms, were established on or near the deep old soils of the southern hills and in some valleys, with the evident objective of growing grain. Near Koiladha bay, a group of small sites was centered on a larger one that today forms a low mound near the bayshore. This village provided, as seems to have been common in the Early Bronze Age, an outlet to the sea, a window on the world; the rich and varied finds we made there attest to its function as an agricultural center. The hills beyond, and perhaps the coastal plain itself, may have remained in use as grazing land. The coast is shown as it was around 2500 B.C. Contour interval 20 m.

cial purposes. The boundary between the Stone Age (Neolithic) and the Bronze Age is thus a matter of definition and convenience, and it should not surprise us that the social and cultural phenomena that indicate a basic change in the mode of living of the people do not always obey such convenient chronological limits.

In the southern Argolid, the first signs that a major change was underway came shortly before the end of the Neolithic, during the last centuries of the fourth millennium B.C. Half a dozen sites appeared across the landscape at that time, sites that we must interpret as evidence for the clearing of woodland and the cultivation of the soil on hilltops and valley floors, in sharp contrast with the long Neolithic years.

The first of these new sites, shown by their millstones, pottery, and stone tools to have been settlements, appeared on the deep soils of the hills south of Franchthi around the middle of the fourth millennium B.C. Other coastal areas followed suit after 3000 B.C.; characteristically, the larger settlements are mostly near the sea. The only exception is on the good soil of the middle Fournoi valley, where a cluster of sites developed quickly into a major and long-lived focus of habitation occupied throughout the Bronze Age, then again in early historical times, and still flourishing today as an agricultural center. Its location well away from the coast is probably due to the fact that in this valley, in contrast to most other parts of the southern Argolid, the deep soils preferred by Bronze Age farmers are absent in the lower reaches near the sea.

Most sites dating to the latest Neolithic and the Early Bronze Age are tiny and have yielded few finds. Since some even lack pottery, our best means of dating, it becomes difficult to say precisely where in the fourth or third millennium they belong, but their distribution is quite clearly related to the best soils of the area. Probably all were small farms or storage buildings near cultivated fields, though some may have been herders' huts. The group across the bay from Franchthi is a good example of such a cluster of small farming sites.

It therefore seems clear that the spread of sites around 5,000

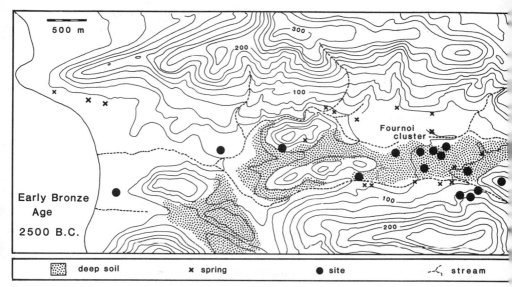

Map 15. Fertile soils on deeply weathered bedrock lie concealed in the heart of the Fournoi valley, northeast of Franchthi. These soils were exploited from a cluster of sites that formed, with its many houses and perhaps 150 inhabitants, the largest village in the southern Argolid at that time. In addition to being an agricultural center, it also seems to have had a monopoly on the manufacture of obsidian tools. The deeply incised Fournoi River presented no flood risk, but water must have been drawn from the many springs that fringed the valley; they are now mostly dry. Unlike most other Early Bronze Age villages in the Peloponnese, the Fournoi cluster was distant from the sea, probably because the soil is not fertile in the lower valley. Evidently, the site was well chosen, because it has remained almost continuously inhabited ever since this auspicious beginning 5,000 years ago. The contour interval on the map is 20 m.

years ago was the result of a need to increase agricultural production that was met by a newly acquired ability to clear woodland and then cultivate it by plowing the deep old soils of hills and valley bottoms. As we have noted before, we do not know precisely when plows were introduced in Greece; pictures of them appear at about this time in the Near East and on Crete. The first evidence for draft animals to pull the plows comes about 2000 B.C. from Lerna, north of Franchthi on the southwestern edge of the Argive plain. It is certain, however, that plows and the animals to pull them would have been nec-

essary to till the hilltop and valley soils deeply enough to insure adequate moisture from the intermittent winter rains for a
crop of wheat or barley. Rain must have irrigated the crops,
because the streams were too deeply incised to permit flooding
of the adjacent soil. Accordingly, we do not, except at Fournoi,
find sites on the valley floors. The little spring-watered meadows near the Franchthi cave apparently no longer sufficed, and
at this time settlement within the cave ceased. The cave became
a shelter for sheep then and has remained so to the present day.

The rain-dependent farming implied by the site pattern
throughout the southern Argolid was probably supplemented
by the pasturing of flocks in the remaining wooded parkland
and on the maquis-covered hills and ranges. It is interesting,
however, that this remarkable expansion did not by any means
include all of the suitable soils. In particular the southernmost
part of the peninsula seems not to have been exploited much,
perhaps because the space was not yet needed or because of the
lack of springs in this area. People must drink, and if settlements are to be located near the best soils, water must be there.
One can, of course, dig a well, and the first of these, some
already 10 m deep, appear at about this time elsewhere in
Greece, but we know of no wells in the southern Argolid that
go back to the Bronze Age. Only much later, in Classical
times, are we certain that the inhabitants of this part of the
peninsula obtained water from wells for their farms and settlements. However, ancient wells are hard to find, because they
tend (rather fortunately for our field walkers) in time to fill
with sediment and so to become obscured.

Though the increase in number of sites is certainly striking,
we need not be overly impressed with its magnitude. After all,
the growth from four sites in the later Neolithic to about 33 in
the Early Bronze Age took more than a thousand years. Obviously, it is not necessary to assume large scale immigration to
explain this; population growth by means of a modest birth
rate would easily suffice. We shall return to that fascinating and
tricky subject, the relation between population density and site
numbers, in Chapter 9.

The sudden blossoming of human culture is not restricted to the southern Argolid but forms part of a more general southward shift of the center of cultural and economic activity involving all of Greece and for the first time also the Cycladic islands. Whereas during the Neolithic very nearly all of the people, and most of the cultural and technological innovation, were found in northern Greece, with the Cyclades remaining largely uninhabited, the Bronze Age brings a great increase in settlements, people, and cultural vitality on many islands, including Crete, as well as along the coast of the Peloponnese. In these places, generally on hills by the sea, the first true towns arose, a network of communications evolved, and a culture came into being of such artistry, liveliness, and sophistication that it is still capable of touching us deeply. In due time, it was to lead to the heights of Minoan and Mycenaean civilization.

The sudden appearance of dispersed settlements in southern Greece, hitherto so sparsely inhabited in comparison with the dense scatter in Boeotia, Thessaly, Macedonia, and Thrace, has generally been interpreted as a southward shift of the population of northern Greece. Some, for example, Colin and Jane Renfrew, have argued that the rise to fortune of the Peloponnese and the Cycladic islands was the result of the introduction of the domesticated olive and grape. This innovation would have made it possible to cultivate marginal lands not well suited for grain or lentils, the kind of land ubiquitous in southern Greece, where good grain-growing soils are scarce.

To us the evidence for cultivation of either the olive or the vine in the Peloponnese and on the islands seems meager until much later, during the Middle or even Late Bronze Age. Early Bronze Age sites in the southern Argolid were always located close to deep soils with the best water-holding capacity, even if that meant abandoning an apparent preference for the coast, and they fit well in an economy based on grain, sheep, and goats. Our view is strengthened by the finding at our sites of numerous heavy millstones, perfect for grinding bread flour, and by the lack there of any of the tools for crushing and pressing olives and grapes.

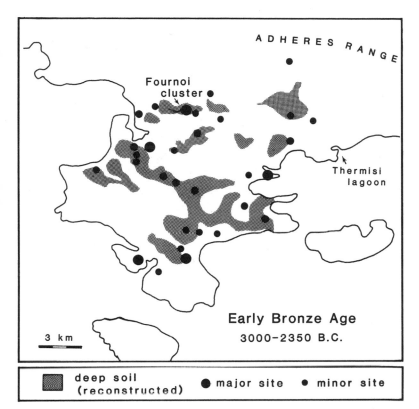

Map 16. The wide scatter of Early Bronze Age sites across the southern Argolid shows clearly just how different the style of life had become from the one that had prevailed for thousands of years. The sites are invariably associated with the best soils but do not by any means exploit all of them. Even toward the end of the Early Bronze Age expansion, a good deal of excellent land remained that had not yet been utilized fully. Around 3000 B.C. we also see a differentiation between sites of different sizes, with different kinds of finds and, evidently, different functions. The first centers appear, each serving a scatter of smaller sites, presumably farms. Of those central villages the Fournoi cluster was the largest and most diversified. The coast is shown as it appeared during the third millennium B.C., and the fertile deep soil cultivated at this time is represented as it was before soil erosion caused by farming reduced its thickness and extent.

The large increase in the number of Early Bronze Age settlements in southern Greece is a fact, yet the fertile plains of the north, though no longer the focus of civilization, were by no means abandoned and continued a slow, steady growth. It does not seem that people migrated south in mass; instead, the evolution in the southern Argolid suggests that the expansion in the south was merely a continuation and acceleration of an indigenous trend that had begun in the Neolithic. If that is so, rather than asking why Early Bronze Age sites are so numerous, we should wonder why those of the later Neolithic are so few. Why, compared with northern Greece, should population growth have begun so late in the south? Of course, we realize that to explain the rise of the Bronze Age in all of southern Greece from the vantage point of the southern Argolid alone is a hazardous undertaking. Nevertheless, the clear continuity from Neolithic to Bronze Age in our area, combined with the lack of solid evidence anywhere for an early major role of olive and grape cultivation, seems to us to argue against the view that those two crops were the catalyst for the southward shift of the cultural and economic center of Greece.

Besides population growth, though inexplicably delayed, there must have been other reasons for the economic and cultural advantages so evident in southern Greece during the third millennium B.C. Perhaps it was trade in woolen cloth that made the sparsely inhabited ranges of the south attractive as grazing lands. The increase in the number of people might have provided the small labor force needed for that activity. The south and the islands also have many more harbors than the north, and that too might have encouraged the economy of the latest Neolithic and the Early Bronze Age when the introduction in the Aegean of gold, silver, copper, and bronze, together with the longboats pictured on contemporary pottery, triggered an expansion of trade. It is only natural that for such a striking event as a major shift of the center of a culture one looks for equally striking causes, but perhaps that is unreasonable; slow population growth, increased trade, and other unspectacular reasons not yet thought of may well have sufficed.

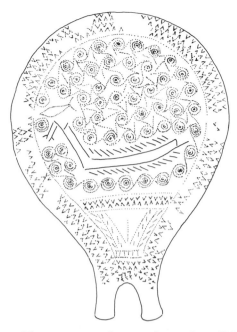

To return to the southern Argolid, growth continued there throughout most of the Early Bronze Age, and the clusters of small sites expanded. Close to each cluster we always find a larger site where wool, grain, and dairy products could be stored, a site most often placed favorably with regard to the coast and perhaps to external markets. By the middle of the third millennium B.C. some of those central sites had advanced to a much higher status than any others. At those main sites, among a rich variety of artifacts, we regularly found remains of houses with fired roof tiles, millstones made of imported andesite, fragments of stone vases and of hearth rims made of baked clay, and a large assortment of smaller items in stone and clay. Fine pottery, distinct from the much more common coarse kitchenware, is also fairly well restricted to these major sites. Even though we collected only from the surface, the central cluster in the Fournoi valley yielded more than 900 sherds, 2,100 pieces of obsidian and flint, and some 55 objects made of ground stone. Most of the imported ware was found at these major sites, which also contained the bulk of the milling and grinding equipment, and so demonstrated their significance as agricultural centers. Except for these few primary sites, all others were small indeed, often yielding no more than a handful of sherds and stone tools, and never any major objects or remains of stone building foundations.

Among the central sites, the villages, the Fournoi cluster stands out for its obsidian industry, then by far the most important toolmaking material. It is there that we found the largest quantities of cores, debris, and flakes anywhere in the area, more than at all other Bronze Age sites in the Ermionis together, showing that obsidian was worked on a large scale.

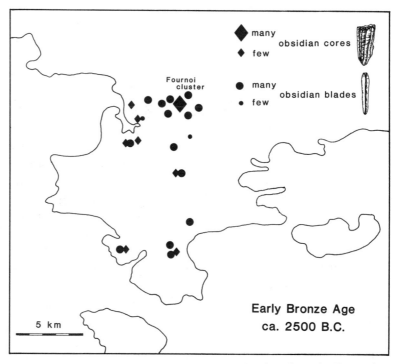

Map 17. Obsidian was worked on a substantial scale only at the Fournoi cluster. There it was converted into blades, knives, sickle elements, and other cutting tools, which can still be found at all other Early Bronze Age sites, both large and small. The residue of the manufacture, however, obsidian cores, is found almost exclusively at Fournoi, where we collected more than 40 cores, compared with just an occasional one at a few sites elsewhere. The coast is shown as it appeared around 2500 B.C.

Blades, on the other hand, the products of the obsidian industry, were found at many other sites, where they were obviously used but not manufactured.

With good justification we can therefore say that, in addition to the farms in the countryside, there were local agricultural centers, and that at least one of those also had a specialized craft industry. Others, to judge from their locations, may have functioned as ports. It is interesting that the obsidian, imported from overseas, was processed at the only major inland site; perhaps we have missed here some additional factor in the system that placed the center of power there.

We may thus distinguish three levels of sites. What should we call them? Are they palaces or major administrative centers, towns, villages, hamlets, or merely different kinds of farms, from large to small, from rich to poor, from powerful to subservient? Sites comparable to our top category have been excavated in the Argive plain at Lerna and elsewhere in Greece as well. They appear to have been small fortified towns, often with one or more large, central buildings, such as the famous House of Tiles at Lerna; we cannot be sure, however, that even the cluster at Fournoi, with its concentration of similar roof tiles, was such a town. Even if it was, we cannot say much about its function: the discussion regarding the purpose of the House of Tiles continues unabated, though most scholars consider it to have been the residence of a powerful ruler or family.

Whatever the precise function of the major settlements may have been, throughout the Early Bronze Age the distribution of sites remains distinctly associated with deep soils, and only a few are found in areas we believe to have been barren and covered with maquis. This pattern is consistent with an economy based predominantly on the cultivation of grains, with at best a subordinate role for pastoralism. Finds from many sites support this conclusion. Millstones and mortars are common, and we have found flint inserts made to fit into wooden sickles, and displaying the typical polish that comes from cutting the stems of grasses or cereals. Occasionally also, grain impressions are found in roof tiles and potsherds of this period, casts mainly of barley, with the odd grain of wheat or oats. The sediments of Thermisi lagoon, laid down at this time, contain pollen of domesticated grains, but virtually none of olive. At the same time, implements associated with the culture of olives, such as press beds, are conspicuous by their absence, and lands later preferred for olive cultivation remained unoccupied.

The greatest expansion of Early Bronze Age settlement came during the middle of the third millennium B.C., and it had a marked effect on the landscape. For tens of thousands of years, ever since the onset of the last glacial maximum, the Argolid landscape had remained unchanged. Its streams were incised, and its slopes stable, neither erosion nor sedimentation being much in evidence, except perhaps along the seashore and a little in the coastal plains. This stability, all the more remarkable because of the drastic changes in climate and vegetation that occurred during those 25,000 years, came to an end late in the Early Bronze Age. Disturbed by the clearing of the natural vegetation and probably by careless plowing, slopes began to fail, and sediments were laid down on the valley floors that indicate massive and sometimes catastrophic soil erosion. These deposits, which we have called the Pikrodhafni alluvium, have been found in the southern Argolid almost exclusively in those valleys and at the edges of those bays where Early Bronze Age settlement and cultivation were most intense. They reflect a considerable, though by no means fatal, loss of good soil. Even today something like half of the original area of this deep soil, though much thinned, remains, a soil that continued to be the mainstay of southern Argolid agriculture for several thousand years more. We shall deal in more detail with the question of land use and soil erosion in Chapter 8, but must now turn to other aspects of the rural Bronze Age economy.

Given the emphasis on trade in our speculations about the Neolithic economy, it is only reasonable to ask whether also in the Early Bronze Age the southern Argolid should be seen as outward looking rather than as deeply absorbed in its own. local livelihood. Obviously, a number of materials, raw as well as finished, were imported. Obsidian, flint, andesite, marble, and perhaps some pottery may have come from the Cyclades and elsewhere, but what was given in exchange is less clear. Metal ores, including copper, occur in small bodies in the Adheres range above Ermioni; they have been mined, mainly for iron, since the middle of the nineteenth century, but there is no evidence whatsoever that these deposits were known in the Bronze Age. Wool may have been exported, but to us the site pattern suggests that pastoralism was of small importance in the third millennium B.C. Olive oil we have already eliminated from consideration. Perhaps, as it was for the ship captains of the nineteenth and twentieth centuries, the area was the home of intrepid seafarers who traded far and wide, bringing back their profits in the form of stone vases and obsidian, or in gold and silver, and weapons and ornaments of bronze. The convenient harbors of the large offshore islands have Early Bronze Age settlements, and good shelter for boats was available near three of the major mainland sites. From such bases boats might have gone out in early summer to trade in the Cyclades, at the head of the Gulf of Argos in Lerna and Tiryns, and in Aegina and Attica perhaps, returning for safe wintering at home each August, when the winds turned bad.

The prosperity of the Early Bronze Age did not last. During the last centuries of the third millennium B.C. an extreme reduction took place in the number of sites, from more than 30 to only one certain and two possible. A large decrease in the population seems a foregone conclusion, and the poverty of the finds on the few remaining sites suggests a deep economic decline, as is in evidence elsewhere in the Peloponnese as well. At Lerna, the House of Tiles was burned, and the signs of upheaval and disturbance can be seen at many sites in the northeastern Peloponnese, on some Cycladic islands, and as far away as Anatolia and Palestine. What caused this widespread disaster a little more than 4,000 years ago has been a matter of much discussion among archaeologists. Though many explanations have been proposed, none is fully satisfactory, but we are inclined to see political upheaval behind the turbulence rather than an environmental cause such as widespread soil erosion of the kind observed in the southern Argolid.

Sparse in the southern Argolid are also the traces of the following period, the Middle Bronze Age. We know of five sites, all placed on top of older major centers, but the scattered farms typical of the previous period are not to be found. The sites are, however, once again adjacent to the deep soils used before, and we may assume that the economic base, grain production and some herding, remained the same. In addition, pollen grains from lagoon deposits suggest that for the first time some olive trees were being cultivated in the area. At all sites the quantity of finds and some architectural remains indicate that prosperity eventually returned after the severe setback near the end of the Early Bronze Age, though to a population of a different origin. The style of their painted pottery, called Middle Helladic, is typical of what is found in the rest of Greece at this time, owing something to the pottery styles of central Greece and even Anatolia for its origin, but being quite unrelated to the pottery of the preceding Early Bronze Age (Early Helladic).

We have talked in considerable detail about the site patterns and finds of the Early Bronze Age to illustrate how one proceeds to weave together local observations and broad regional information from other sources into a plausible but rarely secure interpretation of the past. To continue through the rest of Argolid history in this manner would be tedious and long. Henceforth, therefore, we shall be more concise, trusting that we have said enough about our method to insure that between the simple lines of our conclusions the intricate process that led us there can be discerned.

The number and size of settlements continued to grow throughout the following Late Bronze Age, the time of glory of Minoan Crete, of the Mycenae of Agamemnon and Klytemnestra, and of Homer's Troy. In the southern Argolid, sites near the same deep soils chosen in the Early Bronze Age continued to be preferred, and once again there are many small sites dispersed over the peninsula. The reuse of cave sites unoccupied since the late Neolithic implies a renewed emphasis on herding, and pollen data suggest that olives were cultivated on a modest scale.

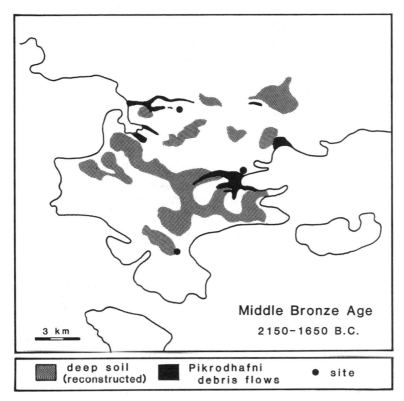

Map 18. Early Bronze Age prosperity came to an abrupt end in the later centuries of the third millennium B.C. All small sites disappeared, and with them probably many of the inhabitants. The remaining population withdrew into three medium-sized villages, each at the location of a former center. The debris flows of the Pikrodhafni alluvium had deposited boulders and mud in valleys adjacent to most former areas of settlement, and much land was deserted. These flows bear witness to considerable soil erosion, due probably to careless land management during the middle and later parts of the Early Bronze Age. The coast is shown as it was around 2000 B.C., and the area of deep soil is given in its reconstructed original extent.

The large storage jars found in every Mycenaean and Minoan palace on the mainland and in Crete leave us with the impression that olive oil played an important role in the palace economy, a view supported by the mention of scented oils in Linear B tablets of the latest Bronze Age. At least in the southern Argolid, however, this image is not confirmed by finds of such essential implements as olive presses. In truth, with a still small population, even the combined consumption of olive oil for cosmetics, food, and light would not require a truly large expanse of olive groves, and the oil, quite possibly from wild trees, was at this time probably used mainly for ointments and perfumes. Therefore we need not yet visualize the southern Argolid covered with so many silvery green trees as stand there today.

In the Late Bronze Age (Mycenaean period) in our area we can recognize several main centers, again close to or on top of principal sites of the Early Bronze Age. Near Franchthi a large artificial mound has long been regarded as the site of the minor Homeric town of Mases. Two other towns occur on prominent hilltops near the sea, one just west of the Classical city of Hermion (Ermioni), the other on the seashore northeast of ancient Halieis. At all three an abundance of Mycenaean finds, including fine pottery, fragments of large storage jars, some characteristic figurines, and architectural remains, testifies to a high standard of living, provincial as these towns may have been compared with Mycenae, Argos, or Tiryns, in the Argive plain farther to the north.

What was the relation of the southern Argolid at this time to the larger Mycenaean units elsewhere in Greece? Do we think of the Mycenaean sites in the southern Argolid as the strongholds of small but independent local chiefs, or were they subject to the control of the better known kingdoms of the Argive plain, as one would infer from Homer's *Iliad*? Attempts by various historians to reconstruct the political geography of these times would align our area with Argos or Tiryns, but those are speculations no one has confirmed. All one should say is that the extreme complexity of the political scene of the southern Argolid in Classical times is a warning not to expect simple answers.

In the thirteenth century B.C. there are indications that the vast Hittite empire in Anatolia began to lose its grip. No longer able to deal effectively with attacks on its borders, it finally broke up around 1200 B.C. A little later, Egyptian records

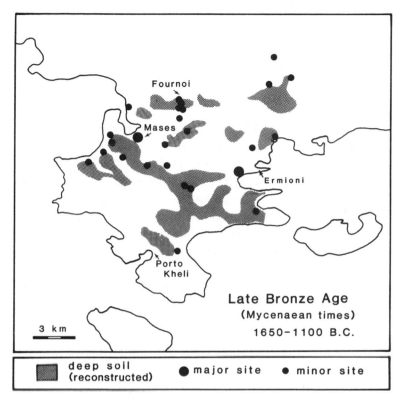

Map 19. During the early centuries of the second millennium B.C. prosperity gradually returned to the southern Argolid, to culminate during the
Mycenaean period. Settlements grew in size and number and spread across
the landscape. Some were larger than any before, and rich finds have been
made on the hilltop site just west of Ermioni, on a small mound at the
shore across the peninsula from Porto Kheli, and on the mound of what
may have been Homeric Mases, near Koiladha bay. Once again, deep soils
were clearly favored but not fully exploited. Evidently, the southern Argolid still had room to spare. When disaster struck once more, the area
became virtually depopulated, and the post-Mycenaean dark age set in. The
coast is given as it was around 1500 B.C., and the area of deep soil is shown
in its reconstructed original extent.

describe an attack by land and sea on the Nile delta by the "Sea
People," a serious invasion that was stopped by Pharaoh
Rameses III around 1186 B.C. These Sea People were appar-
ently a mixed lot, sometimes thought to have included the
"Achaeans" (Mycenaeans?); they may also after their defeat

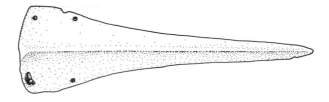

have left the Peleset (Philistines) behind in the Levant, thus giving Palestine its name. The troubles of which the Sea People were but one symptom were felt widely in Greece, and Mycenaean citadels were destroyed or abandoned from Iolkos in the north to Pylos in the southwest.

The destruction that wiped out most Mycenaean palaces in southern and central Greece at the end of the thirteenth century B.C., and struck civilizations across the eastern Mediterranean, Anatolia, and the Levant, left the southern Argolid bereft of all its major and most of its lesser sites. Just four, one of them a fortified mountain top, show signs that habitation continued beyond the fatal date, and even those four are not entirely certain. Clearly, the southern Argolid suffered the same catastrophe that overwhelmed almost the entire eastern Mediterranean. Some people may have lingered in our area for a generation or two; thereafter the survey record fades.

The causes of these widespread upheavals have been much discussed and are still far from resolved. Climatic change has been blamed but cannot be documented; exhaustion of the soil has been suggested, but, at least in our area, later settlers returned to precisely the same lands afterward. Everything else, from invasions to a major economic depression, has been proposed and after lengthy debate rejected. Our own studies provide no independent insight in the great catastrophe, and it is not useful to dwell on it here at any greater length. Rather, we would turn next to the period of renewal that began in the ninth century B.C., after a few hundred years that are a blank in the record of the area.

Chapter 6

·

At the Edge of a
Greater World

After the Mycenaean catastrophe silence fell over the Greek landscape for more than a hundred years. Only a few settlements, most of them carefully placed in secluded areas or on defensible mountain tops, continued to be inhabited, and the interval is properly called a dark age. This dark age of no information conveniently straddles the boundary between the Bronze Age and what in the rest of Europe has long been known as the Iron Age. We do not usually call it that in Greece, because at about this time we also enter the historical period; writing appears in the eighth century B.C., and so simple a term as Iron Age is no longer useful. Nevertheless, this metal-based boundary is a real one, as our colleague Professor Anthony Snodgrass, of Cambridge University, has pointed out. Whereas even in latest Mycenaean times bronze was the metal used for tools and weapons, a tabulation of finds from the tenth century, early in the Iron Age, contains 89 swords, spearpoints, daggers, axes, and knives made of iron, against just eleven of bronze. From then on, bronze was mainly of interest to sculptors; its lack of use for utilitarian purposes has proved unfortunate for archaeologists, because it survives the onslaught of the centuries a good deal better than iron.

In the southern Argolid the dark age was truly that. Within our survey area, we have found no traces of occupation at all until about 850 B.C. or after, well into what is known for its characteristic pottery decoration as the Geometric period. Just beyond the eastern boundary of our area, however, a single coastal hilltop appears to have been continuously occupied from late Mycenaean to Geometric times. Resettlement, when it finally came, was a slow process, and did not begin in earnest until sometime in the eighth century B.C. It was then that the Greeks began to spread out from the Aegean region to settle on the shores of the Black Sea, North Africa, southern Italy, Sicily, and even southern France and eastern Spain in a huge wave of colonization lasting more than 150 years. Population pressure in the towns that had been springing up and growing steadily around the Aegean since the tenth century, especially in Ionia and central and southern Greece, is generally credited with causing this wave of emigrations. Another factor, surely, was the economic revitalization of Geometric Greece through contact and trade with the empires of Egypt and the Near East.

The southern Argolid was close to centers of new growth in the Argive plain, to Athens, and to Sparta, and was located conveniently on shipping routes across the Aegean. Yet it remained largely unoccupied long after colonists from cities in Ionia, Attica, Euboea, and the Peloponnese had begun to swarm in every direction across the Mediterranean and as far as the Black Sea. It is true, of course, that the soils were poor in the southern Argolid compared with such generous lands as Sicily or the shores of southern Russia, and that there was not room for more than a small town or two. But still, room there was, and the soil and climate were much more familiar than those of most other early targets of colonization. Why, then, should a place so close to home have remained sparsely settled for so long at a time when, so it seems, so many were getting on ships and going somewhere else?

In contemplating this question we should remember that, more often than not, population expansion is the result, not the cause, of economic growth and greater prosperity. As the embryonic urban centers in Attica, Corinth, Aegina, and on the Argive plain grew, they required greater and greater quantities of agricultural products for their sustenance. For this need there were two solutions: send some of the population away to found a new city in a country of promise, or look for

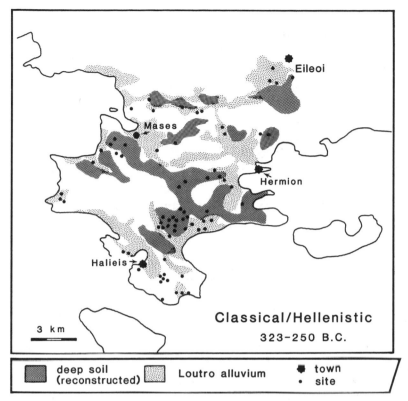

Map 20. In the eighth century B.C., a large expansion of settlement began in the southern Argolid as elsewhere in Greece, reaching its peak during the brief Classical/Hellenistic period. Once again the deep soils were exploited, now to the fullest, but for the first time we also see sites encroach on the old, stony alluvium of glacial age, and on slope deposits that had heretofore been universally shunned. These more marginal lands were suited to the culture of the olive, which demands less water-holding capacity of the soil than grains do. Since olive oil was an excellent cash crop during those years, we are not surprised to see settlements reaching into remote parts of the area, where no one but a shepherd had ventured before. At the same time, some of the villages grew to true towns, such as Halieis, Hermion, and Eileoi. The coast is shown as it appeared between the sixth and the third century B.C., and the area of deep soil is given in almost its original extent, slightly reduced to allow for the effect of the Pikrodhafni erosion phase of the Early Bronze Age.

underexploited land nearby. Since the mother city usually continued to exist and, in most cases, to prosper even after a sizable fraction of its population had left to colonize far shores, the second solution eventually became necessary when the richer but more remote regions had largely been claimed.

Thus it was inevitable that the backwaters of the Greek mainland gradually filled in after the main wave of colonization was over. Adjacent markets, methods of intensified production, and a shift from farming for subsistence to farming for cash crops brought a relative measure of prosperity even to places like the southern Argolid, which did not by themselves have the resources for vigorous economic growth. In addition, many such marginal regions benefited from new needs that prosperity had created in the cities, such as the use of olive oil for food, lighting, and body care. As a result of these different forces a steady expansion of settlement began in the southern Argolid after 750 B.C., followed by slow population growth and increasing prosperity, which continued for many centuries. Most of the pottery left behind by the early settlers is decorated in the style of the Argive plain, and one assumes that they came from that direction. This conclusion is strengthened by the fact that we know that in Classical times the Doric dialect, common to much of the Peloponnese, was used in the Ermionis, pointing to connections as far away as Sparta. Attic pottery, and mythical traditions such as those that have Theseus come from Troizen, may point to colonists from Athens as well.

The evolving pattern of land use becomes clear in the course of the seventh century. Once again we see the familiar small sites located along the edges of the long-popular deep soils of hilltops and valley bottoms, centered in groups on larger villages with more abundant and varied finds. Once again it appears that, at least initially, it was grain that fed the inhabitants of the area, perhaps supplemented by some pastoralism, although the cave sites we have cited before as evidence for herding were not occupied at this time.

Gradually, clear differences developed with the Bronze Age

past. Sparse data from Thermisi and other lagoons show that, beginning early in the last millennium B.C., olive pollen grains become much more common in their deposits, as has been observed elsewhere in Greece also. This increase is so impressive that we are forced to accord to the olive a role in the rural economy of Archaic and later times far larger than what we have deemed likely for the latest Bronze Age. In this connection it is also significant that settlements are now seen to encroach on what were, so far as we can tell, virgin soils. These newly opened lands, progressively more in demand during the sixth, fifth, and fourth centuries B.C., are far from promising at first sight: red and stony soils laid down in valleys by streams and on slopes by slow downward creep over the hundreds of thousands of years of the glacial period. The fields are often steep, and the soils less fertile, holding water less well than the deep soils used in the Bronze Age. The olive, however, is not demanding and, if properly managed by means of terrace walls, behind which soil could accumulate, the newly opened lands would have supported good olive groves, with patches of wheat between the trees. From the seventh century on, site patterns indicate that these soils increasingly came into use, and they are still used today, mostly for this very same purpose.

Thus we surmise that the colonists began by supporting themselves with the traditional grain agriculture, and progressively planted more olive trees until there were enough to permit the export of olive oil. Since olive groves mature slowly, it must have taken generations before the new cash economy reached full flower, as the slow evolution of the site pattern confirms. Initially, the settlers used the best land near the old villages, today marked only by low mounds in the landscape, because the yield of grain was highest there, and because the effort of moving the bulky grain over long distances could thus be avoided. The outlying lands, not by themselves so well suited for cereals anyhow, would serve for the olive, perhaps for grapes, and, of course, for herding.

The extraction of olive oil, however, requires extensive facilities: presses, storage jars for the oil, and quarters, if only sea-

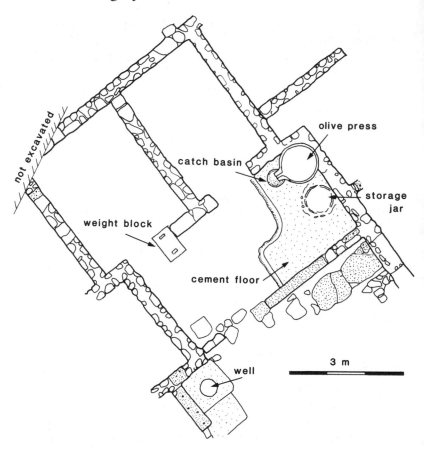

Figure 6. In one room of this excavated Classical house in the lower town of Halieis the inhabitants pressed their olive oil. The equipment, consisting of a press bed, a press (now lost), and a weight block at the end of a beam, was all in one room, with a hygienic cement floor to work on. The oil flowed through a spout into a catch basin and was kept in a large storage jar (pithos) sunk in the floor next to the press. (After a drawing by Thomas Boyd.)

sonally, for the workers. As fields farther and farther away from the villages were opened up for the olive culture, there would inevitably have resulted a wider scatter of sites and the rise of new agricultural centers. Those new centers, if occupied throughout the year, would require food. Because there is a limit to the distance a farmer can walk every day and still do his work efficiently, grain must have been grown among the olive trees, the lower yield and higher risk notwithstanding. This rendered the economy vulnerable, and, should it decline, not only individual farmers but whole villages would have felt the pinch.

This evolution of the rural economy is, we think, what lay behind the origin and growth of the small Argolid towns we know from Classical sources, Mases on the bay near Franchthi and the larger and much better known Halieis and Hermion. Temples were established in the seventh and sixth centuries near Mases on the south flank of the hill that contains the Franchthi cave, and at Halieis and at Hermion on the cape beyond modern Ermioni. From this moment on we can call Halieis and Hermion true towns, the centers of small states, or poleis in the Greek sense, each with its own territory. Mases, on the other hand, remained a local agricultural center dependent on Hermion.

During the fifth and fourth centuries B.C. settlement continued to expand until the number of sites was as great as or greater than it has ever been since. Second-order settlements were established in a pattern well known to economic geographers as the central marketing model. Halieis and a small town of uncertain function above the Iliokastro plateau had orthogonal street plans, unusual for such an early date and more commonly found in colonies remote from the Greek heartland. Both were fortified. Among the smaller sites there were villages and farmsteads, the latter often equipped with towers, as was customary on Greek farms in Classical times. Quite a few sites were more specialized; among these we can identify shrines and sanctuaries.

The events of the Peloponnesian War dominated the later years of the fifth century B.C., a long affair of often confusing alliances and varied fortunes. The greatest growth in the southern Argolid came with the recovery afterward, in the fourth century B.C. Its pattern of farms, villages, and towns is exceptionally clear, and characteristic of this century, because it no longer concentrates solely on the old hill soils, but also on the Pleistocene alluvium in valleys and on the lower slopes, land best suited for the culture of the olive.

Isolated farmsteads now became common, and Halieis prospered and grew to its greatest size. Economic success is also indicated by the fact that we can assign with some degree of confidence about a hundred sites to this time, far more than to any other period except the Late Roman.

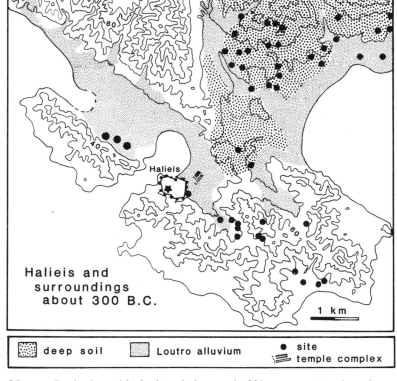

Map 21. Beginning with the late sixth or early fifth century B.C., the culture of the olive took hold especially in the hitherto rather neglected southern half of the peninsula. Focused on the walled city of Halieis with its acropolis (star) and its temple complex outside the eastern gates, the area became a center of olive oil production that put into use all but the most rugged tracts of land. The coast is shown as it appeared between the sixth and the third century B.C. Contour interval 20 m.

Undoubtedly, trade with external markets can be held responsible for most of this affluence, and it is no coincidence that the three lowland towns are located on excellent small harbors. At this time Athens, Corinth, Argos, Aegina, Kalauria (modern Poros), Epidauros, and Sparta may have been potential markets, and the Spartan hegemony after the Peloponnesian War had secured the seaways. The Argolid had a good many products to offer; shipments of purple dye, salt, fish, wool, cheese, grain, wine, and honey, among other things, may have left the ports of Halieis, Hermion, and Mases. The chief export, however, must have been olive oil, as the occupation of so much land best suited to this culture implies, and as is confirmed by the drastic increase in olive pollen buried in the sediments of various lagoons.

Late in the fifth century the Athenians had lost many of their olive trees when the Spartan armies had diligently cut them down. Olive trees need many years to mature and bear their full crop of fruit, and well into the fourth century Athenian olive oil was probably in short supply. Moreover, the population of Athens rose rapidly in the fourth century, and newly expanding cities, Thebes, for example, or Megalopolis, in the central Peloponnese, were located in regions poor in olive groves. Demand must therefore have been at an all-time high; premium prices could be obtained for the oil of the southern Argolid, still highly regarded today, and the region took quick advantage.

Olive pits have been found in the excavation at Halieis, and olive pollen in lagoon sediments, but much more impressive as evidence for a burgeoning olive oil industry are the fourteen press beds and eighteen weight blocks dating to this period that have come to our attention, both in Halieis itself and on farmsteads throughout the area.

Nothing in this world is permanent, however, and certainly not prosperity. In the wake of Alexander, who expanded Greek influence as far as Egypt, India, and Afghanistan, came economic and civil disorders that lasted for at least two centuries. In this Hellenistic period, populations decreased in many parts

of Greece, coasts were ravaged to feed burgeoning slave markets, and military campaigns disrupted trade routes; overall,
there is a good deal of evidence for a decline in the value of
commodities of every sort in the third and second centuries
B.C. The southern Argolid was not spared these adversities.

Accordingly, we see a sharp decline in the number of sites
to only seventeen confirmed ones in the interval that began
around 280–250 B.C. and continued down to the end of the
Roman civil wars in the first century B.C. Halieis, Eileoi, near
Iliokastro, and a substantial village between Halieis and Hermion were abandoned. Mases was reduced to little more than
a landing stage for the ferry to Argos. Much of the area seems
to have become deserted; we have found just a few artifacts
belonging to this period in the formerly well settled Fournoi
valley, on the plain near Franchthi, and in suburban Halieis.
Only the territory of Hermion retained reasonable traces of
the former pattern of villages and farmsteads, but even there a
decline took hold that was still evident as late as the first century A.D. At the same time we find the old cave sites reused,
testimony to a new emphasis on pastoralism, which is less demanding in labor than olive cultivation and less vulnerable to
depredation.

All this indicates a downturn in the economic fortunes of
the region and neglect by the formerly powerful neighbors in
Athens, Argos, and the rest of the Peloponnese. Piracy also was
rampant during the later years of the Roman Republic, when
Greece was a battleground for Roman armies in the civil wars
that ended only with Caesar Augustus's victory at Actium in
31 B.C.

With all those wars and piracy, a long economic depression
was inevitable; it seems to have lasted into the second century
A.D. In the later Hellenistic and Early Roman periods, the inhabitants of the southern Argolid were, once again, reduced to
worrying mainly about their own livelihood. So they turned
their attention inward, to feeding their families, to agrarian
practices less demanding in scarce labor and more likely to
produce a dependable yield, and to settlement sites safe from

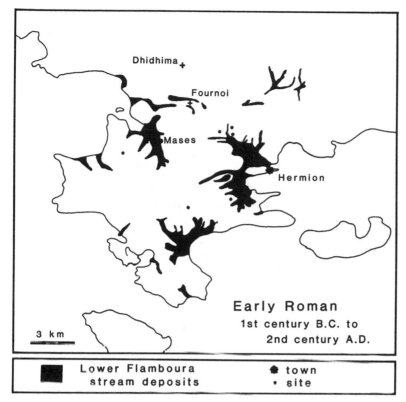

Dhidhima +

Fournoi

Mases

Hermion

Early Roman
1st century B.C. to
2nd century A.D.

3 km

Lower Flamboura
stream deposits

🏠 **town**
• **site**

Map 22. The third century B.C. brought to the entire Aegean world a severe economic depression, which was to last for several hundred years. In
the southern Argolid the reduction in the external demand for olive oil led
to the abandonment of many marginal lands and outlying farms, and to a
withdrawal to soils best suited to the growing of grain. Halieis became
deserted, Mases was reduced to a ferry landing, and only Hermion remained a town, though according to Pausanias a dilapidated one. Reduced
maintenance of slope fields, and the yielding of distant lands to sheep and
goats, caused extensive soil erosion, and stream gravels, sand, and loam of
the Lower Flamboura alluvium blanketed many a valley bottom. The coast
is shown as it appeared during the last few centuries B.C., and for reference
the locations of modern Dhidhima and Fournoi are shown with crosses.

unwanted visits from the sea. A smaller population is prob-able, concentrating on farming only the best lands, lands that would yield grain, and not olives, of which there must have been a considerable surplus for some time until neglect and wilderness took over. Better to make use of those more distant fields by handing them over to the shepherd and his flock; with a minimum investment of money and labor they might still yield a useful return. The shift, however, also did something else, which was surely not foreseen at the time; it led to a con-siderable degradation of the landscape. Maquis took over in many places, as the pollen in lagoon sediments shows, and along the coast pine woods spread for the first time since the post-Mycenaean dark age. At the same time, soil erosion be-came serious, and we have found that the years between roughly 300 and 50 B.C. brought widespread sedimentation, the Lower Flamboura alluvium, a phenomenon that the area had not seen since the later years of the third millennium B.C. We note here that the much more severe depopulation, the virtual desertion, of the land at the end of the Bronze Age had had no such im-pact on the landscape, but we reserve further discussion of the relation between rural prosperity and misfortune on the one hand and soil erosion on the other for Chapter 8.

It was at the end of those worst of times that Pausanias, one of the earliest known writers of travel guidebooks, visited the area. He mentions three villages, and tells us that Hermion, itself now a reduced but recovering town, had new though modest construction and some prosperity, based in part on the Roman peace, on the farming of its fertile valley, and on some manufacture of purple dye. Mases, he says, was only a port for Hermion, a puzzling remark given the small but excellent natu-ral harbor that exists at Ermioni now. Our marine geophysical study, however, lends credence to his words. It seems that the extensive soil erosion of the last few centuries B.C. turned the bay of Ermioni into an unnavigable mud shoal, which became usable again only in the third century A.D., when the sea rose several meters, drowning in the process some of the remains of the old town of Halieis and its temples. That town, by the way, was deserted, and Pausanias did not bother to visit it.

What he meant by the villages is not clear; the three he mentions for our area almost surely included present Fournoi and Dhidhima, but we have found practically nothing there that could be assigned to his time. This points up one of the limits of even the most careful survey, limits we should always keep in mind. The lesson is emphasized by the fact that Pausanias also crossed the Iliokastro plateau and implied that the sanctuary of Demeter there was still standing, even though our survey has turned up not a trace of settlement on the plateau for the first few centuries of our era, except those left by shepherds in Kotena cave, higher in the hills.

Recovery, despite such setbacks as the attacks of the Goths in the middle of the third century A.D., continued and accelerated during the later Roman Empire with the establishment of Constantinople as the eastern capital after the reorganization of the empire by Diocletian and Constantine I, early in the fourth century A.D. The economic improvement was slow at first, until after the raids of Alaric and the Visigoths in 396 A.D., then peaked in the fifth and sixth centuries. A very large number of sites belong mainly to the later centuries of this period, almost as many as we have for the later Classical and earliest Hellenistic time of prosperity. These settlements come in various sizes, and once again there is a hierarchy of farms and villages. Many long-deserted Classical and earliest Hellenistic sites were reoccupied, perhaps because the remains of such buildings as farm towers may have been there to quarry for their stone. A further indication of the new stability of the region is the evident lack of fortifications, even at the larger coastal settlements. It is also quite possible that some of the olive trees, notoriously long-lived and virtually indestructible, were still around to be pruned or regrafted. That would have speeded up the return to high productivity.

Excavations of a Late Roman agricultural villa at Halieis and of an early Christian church and basilica at Ermioni focus the image. The presence of churches at Ermioni, where the ruins of an aqueduct and fountain houses from this period can also still be seen, indicates that this was the principal town of the area at the time. Elsewhere we find country estates like the one

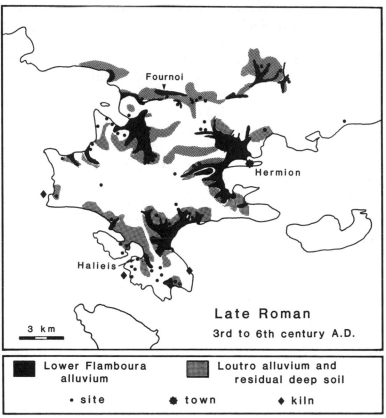

Fournoi

Hermion

Halieis

Late Roman

3 km

3rd to 6th century A.D.

Lower Flamboura alluvium   **Loutro alluvium and residual deep soil**

• site   ⬢ town   ◆ kiln

Map 23. In Late Roman times prosperity returned, spurred once again by an external demand for olive oil. Old sites were reoccupied and numerous new ones were established, some of them near steep, stony lands that had not been used before. The lower valleys, on the other hand, freshly buried under Lower Flamboura alluvium, do not seem to have been attractive, perhaps because their soils were not yet sufficiently mature. Hermion remained the only city, while at the site of former Halieis, and perhaps elsewhere, large agricultural estates arose. At several coastal sites we have found evidence for the manufacture of pottery, tiles, and large shipping jars (amphorae), the last of these probably used for the export of olive oil. The coast is shown approximately as it is now, having made a move landward during a rise of the sea of 2 to 3 m, which began in the third or fourth century A.D.

at Halieis, a traditional Roman *villa rustica*, owned by a farmlord, with its attached population of serf-laborers (*coloni*). The relative comfort of the owners is indicated by the presence of a bathhouse, a facility probably not available to the labor force, whose graves are heartrendingly poor and miserable.

The sites cluster around the same soils that had been used during the fifth and fourth centuries B.C., again with a marked emphasis on alluvium suited mainly for olives. There seems to be some preference for more remote hill country; closely spaced sites are found in upper valleys that had not been exploited intensively before. The impression obtained from all this, that olives were once again the mainstay of the local economy, is confirmed by finds of olive crushers; no fewer than fourteen of the characteristic Roman kind, the *trapetum*, are known to us, some because they still serve as animal watering troughs at wells.

Many Late Roman sites are placed on the coast of the southern Argolid, especially along the southernmost end of the peninsula. As before, we see in the choice of situation evidence for an orientation toward external markets, first of all for the olive oil so obviously the main objective of the rural economy. That, however, was not the only local industry. We have found pottery kilns at several coastal sites, generally on small coves in otherwise apparently empty country. Roof tiles, bricks, and large distinctive globular jars (*amphorae*) were made there in large numbers, and two lucky finds turned up pottery and tiles stacked on what used to be the shore, ready for shipment. They are now barely visible under the waves as a result of a 3 m rise of the sea that began in the fourth century B.C. There is a mysterious aspect to this utilitarian ceramic industry, because we know in the southern Argolid of no deposits of potter's clay of reasonable quality and in quantities sufficient for commercial exploitation; a potter working near Ermioni today imports his raw material from elsewhere. Was the clay shipped in, as it is now, as ballast perhaps, in vessels that were to take the finished products back to the market? But, if so, why build kilns in this area in the first place? Kilns, of course, require

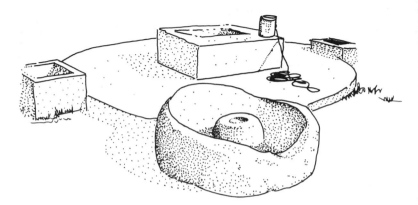

more than clay. Labor is needed, as well as a cheap and abundant source of fuel, and those may have been the factors that enabled the local ceramic industry to compete. Labor tends to be seasonally in oversupply in a region specializing in the culture of the olive, and in the Roman villas labor was cheap. Most important, fuel was available from the maquis on the hills around the kiln sites. The market for the tiles, bricks, and globular *amphorae* was not just a distant one, however. The coves on which the kilns are situated seem to have been chosen with regard to the safe berthing of small vessels of the coastal type, suitable certainly for carrying cargo to Hermion for transshipment, as well as for longer voyages across the Aegean.

What caused this change in the fortunes of the southern Argolid? It is our personal fancy to see here the effect of new trade opportunities arising from the growing fragmentation of the Roman Empire. The safety and unity of the Mediterranean seas had diminished in the second and third centuries A.D. Constantinople had been added as a second capital early in the fourth century, and, after the barbarian attacks of the later fourth and early fifth centuries, the suppliers of grain, wine, olive oil, and, to a lesser extent, mass-produced goods from such remote regions as North Africa or Spain were no longer capable of overwhelming the local competition in Greece. It seems more than likely that the growing fragmentation, political as well as economic, provided new opportunities, rapidly taken by local producers, to serve markets around the Aegean. Even when, in the sixth century under the emperor Justinian I, Roman authority was extended once again over parts of North Africa and Spain, and firmly established in Italy, the more prosperous cities and towns of the eastern Mediterranean continued to provide ready markets for Aegean products. This, however, was obviously an extremely unstable condition and could not last for long, as nothing seems to have done in the economic history of the southern Argolid.

Chapter 7
•
Byzantine Chapels to
Beach Hotels

As we noted in the previous chapter, it should be no surprise that the days of prosperity of the southern Argolid, based as they were on a slow collapse of the old order, were numbered from the moment they began. With the separation between the western and eastern Roman empires now complete, our area was nominally under the control of Constantinople, but the power of the government there to maintain safety and order within its still far-flung borders had already failed occasionally before and declined rapidly during the late sixth and the seventh century A.D.

After the long Indian summer of the sixth century under Justinian I and his successors, the Peloponnese finally felt the fury of the Slavs, Avars, and other barbarians who burst into Greece from the north to ravage and plunder the countryside. No place was safe, except possibly fortified Athens or Corinth. The invaders even threatened Constantinople, and in 808 A.D. the patriarch Nikolaos the Grammarian, a Byzantine historian, wrote: "The Avars had held possession of the Peloponnese for 218 years [since 590 A.D.] and had so completely separated it from the Byzantine empire that no Byzantine official dared put his foot in the country."

At Halieis, a layer of ash covers some of the remains of the late Roman villa, and traces of fire have been noted at other sites, pointing to violent raids as a cause of the abandonment of the Akte. Our latest dated artifacts are coins belonging to the reign of Phokas (602–10 A.D.), found at one of the coastal pottery kilns and at Halieis; after that, nothing. A Slavic raid on Crete in 623 showed that the empire had lost control even of the sea, the economic lifeline of the region, although the Slavs and Avars, firmly settled on the Greek mainland, did not as a rule engage much in seagoing enterprises, being mainly pastoralists. They also generally avoided the low-lying regions, which they may have considered too vulnerable to the same kind of raids that they themselves had carried out.

The southern Argolid was far too small and too exposed to the sea to survive. It also suffered from the fact that once more its external markets had vanished in a puff of smoke. With the means to make a living gone, those of its inhabitants who had not been killed by invasions, pirates, or one of the periodic outbreaks of plague, or hauled away to the slave markets of Egypt and the Near East, left in the hope of a better life elsewhere, and again, as at several times in the past, the area was virtually empty.

Of course, there must still have been the odd shepherd, keeping his flocks out of sight of roving pirates, and an occasional mariner may have looked for water or for shelter against the weather, but we have no evidence that from the middle of the seventh century on there were any settlements left in the area. Gone were the once prosperous Roman villas and remaining small farm communities, while Hermion, last of the towns, must have fallen into ruins. Centuries would pass before life and a measure of prosperity returned once again. The continuity of ancient Greek place names down to the present time, however, shows that some places, like the enclosed and secure Dhidhima valley, were visited often enough to preserve their memory.

When revival finally came in or just after the ninth century, it arrived softly and secretively. Byzantine pottery of the kind used during the tenth and eleventh centuries confirms that settlers arrived in the southern Argolid in the years when the eastern Roman Empire had once again become stabilized and when some prosperity returned to Greece for perhaps 200 years under a succession of emperors starting with Nikephoros I

(802–11). Settlement expanded in many parts of Greece, and the southern Argolid was no exception, but there is an obvious timidity in the choice of sites that suggests that the times were still not as secure as they should have been. Small hamlets and villages are found in the inland valleys behind Ermioni, especially around the Byzantine chapel of Ayia Triadha in Pikro-

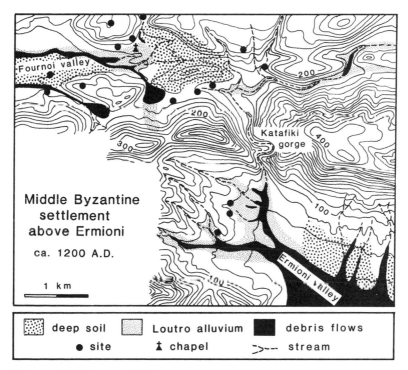

Map 24. The largest Middle Byzantine/Frankish cluster of sites lies well concealed above the Katafiki gorge, east of the Fournoi valley. Today a virtually uninhabited area of olive groves, a few grain fields, and flocks of sheep, in the Middle Byzantine period it contained several hamlets and at least one small chapel or church. The whole cluster seems to have been oriented toward Ermioni, at the time called Kastri, distant some three hours on foot down the gorge and valley of the Ermioni River. The rugged relief of the area is shown with contour lines spaced 20 m apart. During this time extensive debris flows of the Upper Flamboura alluvium washed down from the slopes, quite probably the result of hasty and careless clearing of the land by the new settlers.

dhafni, on the Iliokastro plateau, and in the uppermost Fournoi valley, out of sight of the sea.

The sites are on good arable land, not only on the old upland soils but also on some of the alluvium traditionally used for olives; but they are carefully concealed, tucked away in remote folds of the hills. Other large stretches of the best land, cultivated since the Bronze Age, are not so well hidden, and were not used again until much later. The old town of Hermion, now fortified and known as Kastri ("fortress") was at least partly rebuilt at this time, presumably to provide a link to the outside world. New villages also developed where none had existed before; a cluster of no fewer than eleven sites just east of the Fournoi watershed includes a chapel as well as dwellings and seems to have been a self-contained community. Kranidhi also had its beginnings at this time; first mentioned in an imperial decree of 1288 A.D., it soon became the economic center of the region, perched in safety on its ridge with a commanding view of all approaches.

Early in the thirteenth century the Franks came to the Peloponnese, known to them as the Morea, and acquired as conquerors a little real estate for themselves at the expense of their Byzantine brethren while ostensibly on the way to do God's work in the Holy Land. Some, once safely ensconced in the castles they built on some of the most implausible peaks in Greece, never quite made it that far. From those strongholds they ruled over, preyed on, or defended the surrounding countryside, but one cannot help wondering how anyone having to come down those precipices ever managed to catch a party of marauders or other miscreants. The southern Argolid has two of those spectacular fortresses, both with grand views across the sea. The one on the north coast controlled the Troizenia; the other, near Thermisi, east of Ermioni, was put there, one assumes, to protect the salt industry in the lagoon below, which remained profitable until the nineteenth century. Besides the two fortresses, we discovered the ruins of at least one Frankish chapel, probably not the only Roman Catholic addition to the large inventory of late medieval Orthodox religious buildings, an inventory that looms larger by far than do the sanctuaries in our collection of sites of earlier times. Somewhat later, perhaps in the fifteenth century, the first Albanians settled as retired mercenaries and pastoralists in our area, which they have continued to inhabit ever since. To this very day the Al-

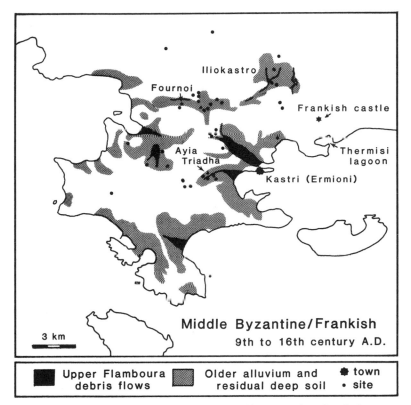

Map 25. Late Roman prosperity was followed by centuries of turbulence, invasions, and depopulation, but settlers returned to the southern Argolid by the ninth century A.D. Characteristically, they preferred inland valleys out of sight of the sea, and the southern peninsula remained largely deserted. Most sites were clustered high above the Ermioni valley, others tucked away in a fold of the land east of present Kranidhi. Careless clearing of the maquis and pine woods that had become established on the deserted fields during the empty years of the dark age resulted in debris flows of the Upper Flamboura alluvium, which once again flooded the lower valleys with mud and boulders.

banian language can be heard there, and people who do not speak Greek or do not speak it comfortably are still quite numerous.

As one might expect when an area is resettled, grain agriculture was given first priority, as is evident from the location of most Middle Byzantine and Frankish sites. Olive culture also fits the nature of some of the resettled lands, and the caves in the hills were used once again, indicating that pastoralism played its part in the local economy. On the other hand, the far southern part of the peninsula, so bustling during Classical and Early Hellenistic as well as Late Roman times, was left untended, as much, we think, for reasons of security as because of its soils, which are less suited for grains.

The colonists may also have grown wine; it suits one's image of Frankish castles, but the archaeological record fails us here, and we have to depend on such circumstantial evidence as place names. Later, cadastral maps prepared by the Venetians in 1705, during their short-lived occupation of the region, show large tracts as vineyards, but it is hard to say how early those were established, or what role the vine played in the local economy and in the lives of the inhabitants.

Unlike the great agrarian expansion of Late Roman times, which was obviously achieved with care for the conservation of the soil, the Middle Byzantine and Frankish settlements raised havoc with the landscape, leaving mud flows in many a valley. We are not too happy with the age limits we can place on these Upper Flamboura deposits, but their occurrence, almost always downstream from the principal medieval settlements, seems to place the blame on careless colonists who cleared away the brush of ages without proper regard for repairing terrace walls or for other means of soil conservation.

One look at the map shows how strikingly the settlement pattern was focused on Kastri (Ermioni), restricted as the sites are to valleys that converge on this coastal town. Such a close relationship to a port raises the suspicion that the shy farmers of the back country were not merely there to feed themselves and their families. Could it be that they provided the salt,

grain, oil, wool, cheese, wine, honey, wax, and perhaps red dye (cochineal) for towns or enterprises elsewhere, on one of the offshore islands perhaps, as was the case in the eighteenth and nineteenth centuries? One would, after all, hardly expect the Frankish garrison in their castle above Thermisi to be capable by themselves of consuming the output of the whole region.

Oddly enough, because we are getting so much closer to modern days, we cannot even begin to answer such questions. It is not wise to project backward from the seventeenth through the nineteenth century into the medieval past to cover the 500 year gap in the written record, broken only by the occasional reference in scattered documents, that exists before we come to the Venetian maps of around 1700 A.D. Strangely also, we have less archaeological information for the period from 1350 to 1800 A.D. than for any comparable interval since the Late Bronze Age, undoubtedly because most of the currently in-habited settlements are on top of their medieval predecessors, and because the archaeological study of coarse pottery and rural farmsteads of this period is in its infancy.

Still, no matter how faintly, one can see resemblances be-tween the settlement pattern of the fourteenth and fifteenth centuries and that of the eighteenth and nineteenth centuries, even though the information for the later period comes from archival sources and may be even more incomplete than the archaeological data. The nineteenth century pattern shows clusters of small sites centered upon agricultural estates belonging to monasteries on the offshore island of Idhra or to Turkish landowners. We know that grain, wine, currants, dairy products, meat, hides, and wool, and also resin, acorns for dye, wax, and cotton, were siphoned off through those estates to support a large population on Idhra, an island engaged during the later eighteenth and early nineteenth centuries in far-flung maritime commerce, with a bit of buccaneering on the side. Such a site pattern, focused on coastal outlets, certainly resembles the Kastri-oriented thirteenth century settlement, and one is tempted to assume that at that time also the agrarian economy of the area served some larger purpose elsewhere. Where, how, and what for, however, we cannot say.

Frustrated by our lack of information concerning what is, after all, relatively recent history, we proceed rapidly past the Venetian and Turkish conquests of the fifteenth and sixteenth centuries, past the Venetian reconquest in the seventeenth, so short it left few traces, past the second period of Turkish occupation in the eighteenth century, which did leave its mark in the form of estate walls, packtrain bridges, and water mills, and arrive at the nineteenth century. It is not our intention to present here an analysis of the most recent history of the southern Argolid, any more than for the previous four centuries, because we are now outside the realm of archaeology and in that belonging to historians, anthropologists, and economists. A brief summary, however, may serve to round out our chronological account.

Since the Greek War of Independence of 1821–32 the population of the southern Argolid has continued to grow, even through nationwide dips during the Great Depression and in the years after World War II, when a continuing exodus to Athens, combined with emigration overseas, emptied many a village elsewhere in the country. The growth rate, of course, has fluctuated, being variously nourished by birth and immigration, the latter mainly of shepherds from Arkadhia, in the central Peloponnese. In parallel with the population growth,

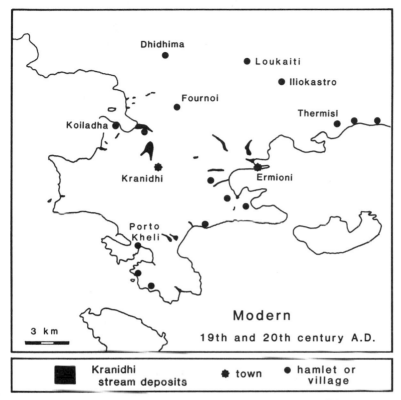

Map 26. The present settlement pattern of the southern Argolid is similar to that of several stages of the past. Many of the hamlets and villages are on or near ancient sites occupied since the Bronze Age (for example, Fournoi and Ermioni), or at least since Classical times (Dhidhima). Others are new and speak of the rearrangement that took place in the Middle Ages, probably for security reasons. Kranidhi, grown from a small cluster of Middle Byzantine hamlets, is one such new town, now the commercial center of the area. Others are younger still, Porto Kheli, for example, or Iliokastro. The vagaries and vicissitudes of land use in the past several hundred years, and the present orientation toward new crops such as citrus and tomatoes, have produced spotty soil erosion on a small scale that began several hundred years ago in the Fournoi valley, and that continues vigorously today in the lower Ermioni valley.

the number of settlements has increased as the central town of Kranidhi, still today the place where one goes for shopping, banking, or to catch the bus to distant parts, has lost people to the coastal towns of Porto Kheli, Koiladha, and Ermioni. As a result, the site pattern today rather resembles that of Classical and earliest Hellenistic or Late Roman days, and for much the same reason.

The key to today's economic good fortune is to be found in the unusual growth of the area in recent years, in contrast to the decline of most of rural Greece. This growth can be attributed to the ability of the local citizens to tap once again into markets in adjacent areas, in rather the same fashion as in Classical and Late Roman times. We should know more, however, about the nature of those modern external markets than we do for those of the remote past, and so, if enlightened suitably by studies in economics, social geography, and anthropology, we should be able to answer some interesting questions. Is it, for example, the growth of Athens by itself that has stimulated the unquestionable prosperity of the southern Argolid? Or would that not have been sufficient, had not the growth of an international European economy, in which Greece has had a part, created broader opportunities? Alas, we are out of our depth here, and have little work by others to draw on, but that need not prevent us from stating the questions. The answers will emerge later.

Apart from a thriving tourist industry, surely on this scale a phenomenon new to history, the southern Argolid has managed to develop a large array of activities, including pastoralism, grain-growing mostly for local consumption, the production of wine, olives, and citrus, market gardening of tomatoes and vegetables, fishing, seafaring, and small-boat building, land sales, trade of many kinds, and, an important element in the fiscal balance, remittances sent by natives now living and working abroad. How did all this come about in an area that might equally well have turned to an ever more isolated existence focused on mere survival?

Susan Sutton, of Indiana University, one of our anthropological colleagues, believes that the lively maritime trade immediately after the War of Independence was the crucial factor
that caused the inhabitants of the southern Argolid to orient
themselves outward. That process was not new; it was nothing
more than the eighteenth and nineteenth century activity on
Idhra or Spetsai transferred to the mainland that once furnished those islands with food, while learning its lessons in the
meantime. It set up a system of external links, a network of
trade contacts that, as soon as a local surplus became available
through population growth and intensified agriculture,
allowed its distribution to the outside at a profit. Today, the
distant look in the eye, this orientation toward profits based on
external demand, sometimes from far away, continues to infuse
the economy of the area and makes it more than just a rural
backdrop to a play that is acted out on a stage elsewhere. How
long it will last as the inhabitants ever more turn their efforts
and products toward feeding and entertaining the tourist
crowd is another matter, but it is evident from our story that
the area has weathered many ups and downs over the millennia, and has shown a remarkable resilience after each setback,
no matter how major. We cannot lay this resilience at the door
of some special quality of the people, however; most Greeks
living there now are not even remotely related to the people
who settled the countryside over and over again during the
past 50,000 years. It must therefore be something in the clear
Greek air, or perhaps it is the geographic setting. Let us be satisfied for the time being with this simple and slightly romantic
answer.

Chapter 8

•

Learning to Take Care
of the Soil

The southern Argolid is a land made mostly of stone. What little soil is perched precariously on its slopes is in constant danger of washing down into the valleys or ending up on the sea floor. Essential to man's survival, the soil is easily damaged by the farmer's use and lost to the sea forever. It is now time to pull together the hints scattered throughout previous chapters that rural economics, human history, and soil erosion are closely connected. That should lead to our own answer regarding the age-old question whether it was man who is to blame for the barrenness of the land, or nature, with or without his help.

Over the eons, rocks exposed at the surface break down and weather to form soil. Heat and cold, rain and drought, the roots of plants, and animals living below the surface do the work that turns what once was limestone, shale, or ophiolite into a soil in which plants can grow and archaeologists dig. Vegetation and burrowing organisms enrich with humus the top layer, which the farmer exploits. When it rains, water seeps down into the soil, dissolving some minerals, and precipitating others a few tens of centimeters farther down, where they slowly form a brown to red clayey, blocky layer. Where the summers are dry and hot, the water retained in the soil after the winter rains evaporates from a little deeper still, leaving behind a prominent white calcareous hardpan. Soil formation is slow in the dry climate of the Mediterranean; a fully developed soil, strikingly red in color and with a hardpan like a limestone

bank, takes tens of thousands of years to form. Still, even embryonic soils, perhaps only a few thousand years old, are quite
distinct in character, and we can use the different degrees of
soil maturity to assign approximate ages to them. Those ages
can be calibrated with archaeological finds or dating techniques based on the decay of radioactive carbon, or uranium
and thorium. By such means we have been able to identify in
the southern Argolid seven separate periods of soil formation
during the past several hundred thousand years.

Soils formed by weathering are not the only young compo-
nents of the Argolid landscape. In valleys and on coastal plains,
sediments supplied by erosion and slow creep downslope have

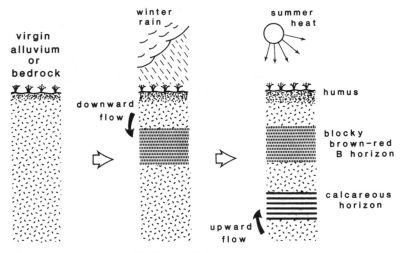

Figure 7. In the semi-arid climate of the Mediterranean, soils form on
any suitable substrate, be it alluvium or bedrock. Humus accumulates in
the surface layer as a result of plant growth. Downward percolation of
rainwater in the winter, fortified with carbon dioxide and acids derived
from the humus, dissolves minerals in the upper zone, only to precipitate
them farther down as a dark brown to red, blocky, clayey layer. The summer heat causes groundwater to rise and evaporate, leaving behind, a little
deeper still, a bank of calcareous nodules. Over time both the brown or red
clayey B horizon and the calcareous bank become denser and more conspicuous, permitting us to distinguish old, mature soils from younger, less
evolved ones.

formed deposits that are the youngest members of the geological sequence in the area. To a first approximation we can guess their ages with the help of the soils developed on them. These ages must then be confirmed by radiocarbon dates from wood or charcoal enclosed within the deposits, or by means of enclosed artifacts and archaeological sites buried by or established on top of them.

At the present time, not much sedimentation takes place in the valleys of the southern Argolid, because the streams are deeply incised and seldom flood their banks. Even when they do, during heavy winter rains, they carry but a little loam to the sea, leaving their channels floored with boulders and gravel, which today seldom move at all.

This has not always been so. A keen observer, if possessed of a mind that is able to see simple patterns in complex observations, would note that all over the Mediterranean there seem to be two kinds of deposits: older ones that are often bright red, and younger ones brown or gray in color. It is also obvious that most streams have incised beds and thus are incapable of depositing the layers of sediment that can be seen to cover ancient ruins, some as young as Late Roman times. Evidently, the present stream regime has alternated from time to time with another, when soil washed into the streams from unstable slopes and filled their channels with gravel and sand, while loams were deposited far across the plains.

Some fifteen years ago, Claudio Vita-Finzi, a geologist who has spent much time in the Mediterranean, came to just this conclusion. The two kinds of soils, old and young, red and brown, seemed to him to imply that there had been two periods of deposition, as well, one long ago during late glacial times, the other very recent, after the Romans had built their towns, walls, and dams. He attributed both to changes in climate, the first to glacial conditions, the second to a more recent time of cold, wet weather known as the "Little Ice Age." It was a simple concept, attractive because it seemed to apply all over the Mediterranean, and archaeologists have used it repeatedly to reconstruct the landscapes of the past for their surveys or around their excavations. Unfortunately, further work has shown that the scheme is too simple, and hence in many cases misleading.

We too needed to understand the history of the landscapes inhabited by the people who left the sites we hunted down with so much effort, but rather than apply a predetermined scheme we studied the late Quaternary landscape without preconceptions. The results were pleasantly clear-cut but showed that, in our area, the slopes had become unstable, the rivers had ceased to incise, and alluvium had blanketed the lowlands not twice but no fewer than seven times. Each time the instability and alluviation were brief, lasting from a few thousand to as little as a few hundred years, whereas the intervals when erosion was negligible and the streams cut their channels deeply below their banks had been much longer. During these long times, soils developed on the slopes and valley floors, and loam was on rare occasions deposited on the flood plains, but otherwise the land was stable for thousands of years.

Not all seven alluvial deposits formed in the same way. Some are a chaotic mass of boulders, cobbles, and sand, mixed with silt and clay without any sign of the sorting and bedding that are usual in streams. Others are well sorted and cleanly bedded, invariably becoming finer in an upward sequence from cobbles to gravel to loam. This kind of alluvium still forms as stream deposits in our area whenever a river flows fast enough to sort the sediment by size, depositing the gravel where the flow is rapid, the loam where the water is still. The other type does not seem to form in the southern Argolid at the moment, but elsewhere other geologists have observed how the mantle of weathered debris on a slope, from boulders to silt, may come down in a mass, too fast and too copiously for the stream to sort and deposit neatly segregated beds of sand and gravel. Such debris flows, halfway between a mud avalanche and normal stream transport, are produced when slopes catastrophically fail or when the rain erodes them in sheets rather than, as normally happens, by means of gullies.

As it turned out, some of our seven alluvial deposits consisted mainly of debris flows, and others of stream deposits,

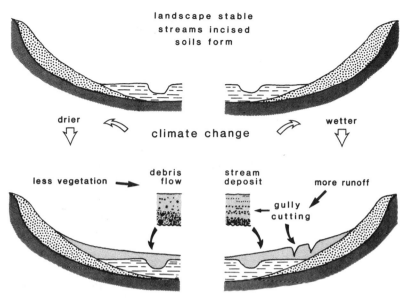

Figure 8. Soils (pattern of large dots), even when perched on slopes, are protected from erosion by the plant cover. A change in climate may weaken this protection, especially if it is sudden, and even if it is only temporary. Should the climate turn drier, plants may wither, and whole sheets of soil may wash downslope to be laid down in the valley as sometimes catastrophic debris flows. A turn to a wetter condition, on the other hand, strengthens the vegetation, but also leads to more runoff. This increases vertical erosion in gullies and upstream channels, and causes stream gravels, sands, and loams to be deposited on the valley floors. Human activity mimics nature by clearing slopes and by concentrating the natural runoff around buildings and along paths to erode channels where none existed before. The bedrock of the valley and slopes is shown with a dark shading, and an already existing valley fill is indicated with horizontal dashes.

but each ended with a thick loam, slowly formed during long years of stability on the rare occasions when the stream, once again incised, overflowed its banks.

Three of the alluviation events in our sequence are old and together form the equivalent of Vita-Finzi's older fill. They were laid down at various times during the later Ice Age, presumably because of changes of climate that affected plant cover and runoff. After the last one the landscape remained stable for 25,000 years, until about 4,500 years ago, when the pace of landscape evolution suddenly quickened. Since then the stability of the slopes and the regime of incised streams have been interrupted no less than four times by soil erosion and the deposition of sediments in valleys and plains. It can hardly be accidental that this abrupt change in pace coincided neatly with the first major expansion of human land use.

In previous chapters we have suggested that what caused those later events was not repeated climatic change but the farmer's casual way in dealing with the soil. It is now time to examine that suggestion more carefully. As we do so, however, it is well to remember that we have little more than our own data to go by, that what we believe flies in the face of the cherished ideas of others, and that the story about to be told, though probably true in the southern Argolid, may not be so anywhere else.

The stability of the landscape of the southern Argolid is maintained naturally by the vegetation or artificially by soil conservation. It can be upset when a change of climate decreases the plant cover or increases runoff, or by a failure of soil management. In a Mediterranean climate, however, the natural vegetation tends to recover quickly after a disturbance, provided that there is no persistent overgrazing, excessive brush cutting, or frequent setting of fires. Quite often we have seen fields that, cut by bulldozer on steep slopes but having failed to deliver the anticipated harvest, are now densely grown with maquis, just a few years after abandonment. Such a capacity for revegetation suggests that political adversity, or an economic downturn so severe that a large part of the land is entirely abandoned, would not result in much soil erosion and would therefore leave little trace in the geological record. This fits well with the observation mentioned in Chapter 5, which then seemed rather astounding, that the apparently complete depopulation at the end of the Mycenaean period left no geological record at all.

The destabilization of slopes and soils, accompanied by alluviation in the valleys, can take several forms. Every settlement disturbs the soil and the vegetation. If people build their

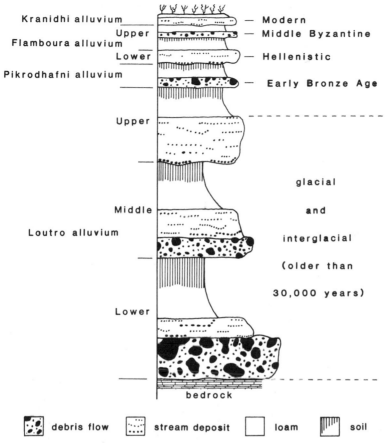

Kranidhi alluvium — Modern

Upper — Middle Byzantine
Flamboura alluvium

Lower — Hellenistic

Pikrodhafni alluvium — Early Bronze Age

Upper

glacial

Middle and

Loutro alluvium interglacial

(older than

30,000 years)

Lower

bedrock

debris flow   stream deposit   loam   soil

Figure 9. Seven times during the last several hundred thousand years the
equilibrium of the southern Argolid landscape was disturbed by erosion of
slopes and sedimentation in valleys. Sometimes debris flows carried away
the soil mantle that had slowly accumulated over the ages, while at other
moments higher runoff eroded gullies and channels and left a blanket of
stream deposits in the valleys. During the far longer intervening times,
however, the landscape was stable, and red soils and thick calcareous horizons slowly matured. The degree of soil maturity is indicated in this dia-
gram by the length of the vertical shading of the loam horizons. Three
alluvial deposits and three mature soils formed before man began to inter-
fere seriously with the landscape. Four more deposits and three soils—the
latest loam being too young to possess an identifiable soil—date from
the past 5,000 years, since the beginning of the expansion of settlement in
the Early Bronze Age. Probably, the hand of man is to be seen in this
sudden acceleration of the slow processes of erosion and sedimentation.

dwellings on a ridge or hilltop, the action of human and animal feet and the channeling of runoff by structures, trails, or streets will cause deep gullies to be cut on the slopes below, exposing bare rock all around the settlement. The effect is strikingly illustrated by the furrowed, barren slopes below the hilltop town of Kranidhi. The sediment, of course, must go somewhere; a large fan of Byzantine and later deposits in the plain of Koiladha bears testimony to the erosive power of the town of Kranidhi above.

Prehistoric examples are equally easy to find. On the ridge south of Koiladha perches a row of Bronze Age sites from which large areas of deep upland soils were once exploited. Erosion has stripped those soils away in the immediate vicinity of each site, leaving it sitting on and surrounded by barren bedrock, as Kranidhi does today.

More important are two other forms of soil erosion. Sheet erosion produces the characteristically coarse, chaotic debris flows that can, during a single event, fill a valley with deposits several meters thick, and leave entire slopes stripped bare of soil. Vertical erosion, on the other hand, cuts deep gullies that converge downslope, concentrate the runoff, and yield sorted, stratified stream deposits in the valley below. The sediments created by these two processes are quite distinct and allow us to draw confident conclusions regarding the causes of the destabilization of the landscape.

Even without deliberate conservation, Argolid soils on the gently rolling hills and in the wide valleys exploited throughout the last five millennia are not especially vulnerable to erosion, as is evident from the fair proportion still remaining after more than 5,000 years of exploitation. Moreover, prehistoric farmers tended to use a field for only one or a few harvests, afterward leaving it fallow to regain its fertility over several years. The longer the fallow, the larger would have been the area interspersed between plowed fields that had been unused for some time and that hence was protected by a growth of maquis. This equilibrium may be upset by a series of unusually wet years, especially if the rains should occur in the summer or early fall, during or just after plowing and before the new crop has greened. Such minor climatic variations are common enough and have sometimes been invoked as a handy explanation of last resort when nothing else will account for some historic or prehistoric event. Unfortunately, they leave few if any traces in the geological record, are impossible to prove, and do not provide us with a useful hypothesis here.

If a growing population demands more food, the quickest way to provide it is to shorten the fallow. That, however, increases the proportion of land freshly plowed and thus enhances the risk of soil erosion. So does careless, rapid clearing of new fields, especially on slopes. In extreme cases, such practices may bring a quick penalty of soil loss, most likely by sheet erosion or catastrophic slope failure, followed by the deposition of debris flows on the fields in the valley.

Twice, events of this type have upset the landscape equilibrium of the southern Argolid. The first took place, as we have seen, in the Early Bronze Age but, although serious, was not extensive enough to be called a true catastrophe. It came long after agricultural expansion began in the latest Neolithic, and therefore cannot be convincingly attributed to the initial clearing of the woods. We do not know whether the debris flows now found in the valleys below the main settled areas of the Early Bronze Age were all formed at the same time, but if they were, a series of abnormally wet summers might be invoked to explain the disaster. On the other hand, if they were laid down separately over a longer time, several centuries perhaps, one would rather attribute them to human activity alone. In that case, a reduction in fallow would be a sensible explanation, thus making the event the delayed consequence of almost a millennium of neglect of even the most minimal soil conservation.

The second instance of sheet erosion or catastrophic slope failure probably came during the Middle Byzantine reoccupation of the southern Argolid, after the empty years of the seventh through the ninth centuries. Fields densely overgrown with maquis since their Late Roman abandonment seem to

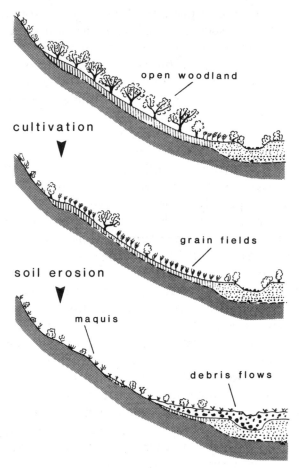

Figure 10. During the Early Bronze Age large tracts of hill country and valley bottom were gradually converted to farmland. As steeper slopes were cultivated and the proportion of fields left fallow for some years was reduced, the risk of soil erosion increased. Finally, either intensified use or perhaps a few years of unusually heavy or unseasonal rain caused extensive soil erosion, and debris flow deposits were laid down in the most densely inhabited valleys. Bedrock is shown with a dark tone, and the soil mantle on the slopes with vertical shading. A previous stream deposit is indicated with a dotted pattern.

have been rapidly cleared with little thought for the reconstruction of the terrace walls that had enabled previous farmers to use the land without risk. Things were made worse by the fact that most of the newly cleared fields were located in the headwaters of streams and included many steep slopes, some never exploited before. Consequently, the loss of soil was larger than that in the Early Bronze Age. We have therefore two cases of major soil erosion, with similar but subtly different causes: rapid clearing as opposed to intensified use, both without proper attention to soil conservation.

Many techniques exist to counter the loss of soil in hilly countries with highly variable rainfall and runoff. In the Mediterranean, the one almost universally applied combines slope terraces with check dams across gullies and small streams. It is very effective in reducing sheet erosion, and in addition gathers any soil still washing down from the slopes above. If kept in good condition, such terrace walls and dams almost completely prevent gullying and loss of soil. On the other hand, the soil reservoirs that accumulate behind those structures are delicately perched on their slopes. Should decay of the terrace walls set them in motion, they will not stop until they have reached the valley floor, the loss of soil on the hills can be large, and the damage on the valley floor devastating. An excellent technique for landscape management, terracing exacts a price of unceasing maintenance. Interestingly, in view of the millennia of Greek experience with terrace wall and check dam construction, most of those we have seen were neither well designed nor well built, certainly not when compared with the splendid structures one sees, for example, in the high Andes of Peru. Probably it is cheaper in times of prosperity to keep repairing the walls than to invest in more durable but costly initial construction, especially since the seasonal rhythms in a country where the wheat harvest comes early leave time for such chores in other parts of the year.

Terracing was first introduced in the Levant late in the Bronze Age, probably together with the culture of the olive. In the Argolid, Classical and later inhabitants used slopes so steep that

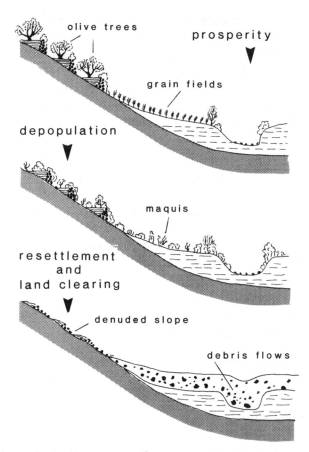

Figure 11. In the Mediterranean, when prosperity is followed by complete depopulation, nature takes over, and maquis and pine woods quickly stabilize the Aegean landscape without allowing serious erosion to occur, as was the case during the post-Mycenaean and early Byzantine dark ages. Such recolonization takes at most a few decades to be complete. Hasty, careless clearing of the vegetation, when the population returns centuries later, may abruptly release the store of soil on the slopes, as apparently happened during the Middle Byzantine revival. Once again, the results are a major loss of soil and the devastation of bottom lands by debris flows. Bedrock is shown with a dark tone, and previous valley fill with horizontal dashes.

only terracing would have allowed the exploitation of the thin, sloping soils. Few terrace walls so old have been identified in Greece, but this may be because their construction has changed so little with time that we cannot tell the difference between a Classical (or even Neolithic) wall and a modern one. One might scrabble in the accumulated soil behind them in hopes of finding datable sherds, but that would depend on sheer luck and is unlikely to please the landowner. Occasionally, however, we have found in terrace deposits a soil profile that could be several millennia old. Without a doubt, Mycenaean engineering, capable of building dams, bridges, and roads, was up to the task of terrace construction, but we do not know with certainty of any Mycenaean terrace walls. Nevertheless, it is reasonable to suggest that the long period of landscape stability following the Early Bronze Age erosion phase and lasting until the last few centuries B.C. was due to the introduction of terracing by the Mycenaeans.

Somewhat counterintuitively, total abandonment of a terraced landscape need not have serious consequences at all, even though there are, up there on the slopes, those vulnerable reservoirs of soil ready to wash down into the valley. The paradox is due to nature's vigor. In any modern Argive landscape one can see wood hedges of pistachio, wild pear, prickly kermes oak, and other shrubs, which adorn the edges of even fully cultivated terraces. Should such a terrace be abandoned, the shrubs and their roots continue to provide a natural retaining wall even after the stones of the artificial one have tumbled down and nothing but an embankment of soil remains in the landscape.

Partial abandonment is a different matter. During an economic downturn, the farmer, concerned to save money, may decide that grain is best grown on his good bottom land, and that his olives will survive for a while without much maintenance of their terraces. It may then seem a good idea to let the shepherd roam the marginal lands, so that at least some small measure of profit can be squeezed from them at little cost, apart from what the olives might still yield. But the cost, as it turns out, is not little. Herding on a terraced slope requires much care to prevent the flocks from damaging the walls as they climb up and down the slopes. Hence, shepherds today can often be seen constructing barriers of thorny branches, and they sometimes repair and reinforce walls and dams as well. When, however, the landowner loses interest in the maintenance of his property, the shepherd is not likely to remain so industrious as before, either.

Two things then happen, usually quickly, both of them bad, sometimes even fatal for the soil accumulated over centuries. First, sheep and goats begin to make trails across the terraces, kicking stones down where they clamber over walls. Runoff, channeled down those paths, soon excavates deep gullies, which branch out behind the walls and rapidly remove much of the stored soil. Simultaneously, the check dams that were meant to control the flow in existing gullies and streams are undercut and collapse. Those dams, like the terrace walls, tend to be constructed in a rather happy-go-lucky manner, probably, again, because maintenance is deemed more convenient than elaborate initial construction. Two almost universal flaws of dam construction in the southern Argolid are the lack of a good lip for the overflow and the absence of a reinforced splash-basin below. As a result, one can frequently see the dilapidated stubs of broken dams clustered together in a stream cut, all fallen because of the same construction defects, all patiently rebuilt in the same faulty manner. The general decay, leading to scatters of stones across the slopes and to branching systems of deep, steep-walled gullies, is hastened by the common practice of cutting the brush on terrace edges for fuel, fences for sheepfolds, and fodder.

The subsequent erosion can be rapid indeed. In a small valley south of Koiladha, intact terraces can be seen on aerial photos taken in 1961, but in 1979 only a few stretches of wall remained, the slopes were covered with scattered boulders, deep gullies had formed, olive trees had fallen, and nearly a foot of new alluvium had accumulated on the valley floor.

In the southern Argolid, the last 4,000 years have provided

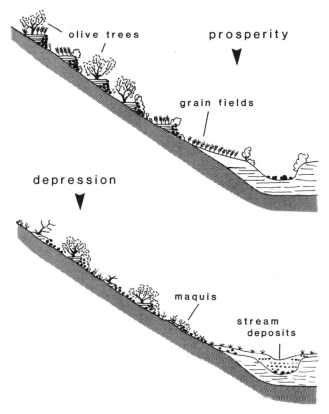

olive trees

prosperity

▼

grain fields

depression

▼

maquis

stream deposits

Figure 12. Prosperity brings with it the urge to exploit marginal lands for cash crops. It demands, and can afford, measures of soil conservation that, in the Mediterranean, usually consist of the construction of terrace walls and of check dams across gullies and stream channels. If properly maintained, these walls and dams effectively forestall soil erosion. Should an economic downturn arrive, however, their maintenance may be considered too expensive: the farmer may withdraw to more fertile fields, and the terraces and slopes are yielded up to the shepherd and his flock. The protective vegetation is then damaged by grazing, walls are trampled, and brush is cut. Runoff excavates gullies along animal trails, the flow of rainwater becomes concentrated, and the precious soil of the terraces washes away to cover the bottom lands in the valley with stream deposits. Bedrock is shown with a dark tone, and previous valley fill with horizontal dashes.

us with two examples of this type of soil erosion, of which the later is the more instructive, because we can still see it in progress. The recent neglect of terraces obvious in many parts of our area is not due to economic stress so much as to changes in the owner's economic interests. He may have decided to sell his land for development as summer-house lots, he may no longer be keen on growing his own food, or perhaps he plans to use his energies in the tourist industry rather than on the farm. Nevertheless, the results closely resemble those of a regional economic depression, although on a more limited and local scale.

The recent alluvium, its age a good deal less than a thousand years though often not precisely determined, is thin and rather scattered throughout the area, and it records a varied history of terrace neglect and slope gullying at different times in different places. The Fournoi valley, after a brief spell of soil erosion probably a few hundred years ago, has since remained stable, protected by its old and profitable olive culture. In the Ermioni valley, on the other hand, soil erosion started only a few decades ago, because one finds pieces of plastic embedded even in the lowest layers of the deposits. At the present time, sedimentation continues there, fed by the rampant stripping of the valley slopes by bulldozers cutting terraces where they once were built up. Demonstrating how rapid this process can be, a deposit several meters thick has been laid down in the lower Ermioni valley in less than 40 years. Evidently, the various modern erosion events, although all of the same kind and due to similar causes, are related to very localized and often brief changes in economic fortune.

A widespread economic decline affected the Hellenistic and Early Roman economy in the eastern Mediterranean and had an impact in the southern Argolid as well. At the same time, a gully erosion event took place, quite precisely dated to the last few centuries B.C. (ca. 250–50 B.C.). Like its modern counterpart it was rapid, but it took place almost simultaneously over the entire southern Argolid, and left much thicker and very much more extensive deposits behind. Such stream deposits might conceivably indicate a turn of the climate toward more rainfall and thereby suggest a climatic cause for the economic downturn, but there is no independent evidence for a climate change either in our area or in the Aegean in general.

The changing settlement pattern in Hellenistic times points in the opposite direction. It was, we think, not nature that caused an economic depression, but an economic depression that brought erosion and alluviation in its wake. A comparison of the settlement pattern of the fourth century B.C. with that of the following centuries shows that, presumably as a result of the economic downturn, the later Hellenistic and earliest Roman sites contracted into much smaller districts than before. This led to the abandonment of large outlying tracts too expensive to maintain, and perhaps also of some coastal ones judged to be too exposed to pirates. Most of these tracts had been extensively cultivated during the preceding period of prosperity and would have been harmlessly colonized by pine woods and maquis had they been left alone. Apparently, however, many of them were turned over to pastoralists, with all the consequences we have described above. This did extract some continuing monetary return, but at the same time it prevented maquis and pine woods from stabilizing the landscape, and so, in the long term, led to the largest soil losses that can be attributed to human influence in this area.

The recent landscape history of the southern Argolid thus appears to be closely correlated with human events. During the last few hundred thousand years slopes were eroded, and bright red alluvial deposits accumulated in the valleys, but the process was intermittent, with very long periods of quiescence in between. The minuscule human occupation in the Neolithic failed to alter the present landscape because so little was exploited, and most of the arable fields of that time are now anyhow probably beneath the sea. The long stability came to an end in the third millennium B.C. with extensive slope failures that led to the deposition of debris flows in the most densely inhabited valleys. The cause, we believe, was a gradual decrease in the area of fallow fields, perhaps assisted by the clearing of ever more marginal lands, although a period of heavy summer rains cannot be entirely ruled out. The experience was not in vain, however, because about 2,000 years followed during which the land remained stable, even when it emptied out totally, during the post-Mycenaean dark age. This stability suggests that soil conservation had been discovered and successfully practiced probably as early as the later Bronze Age.

The system broke down shortly before the end of the last millennium B.C., probably not because of a change in climate but through the inherent vulnerability of the terrace method of soil conservation. Stability was restored soon by colonization with maquis and pine woods, and during the Late Roman period of prosperity the lands were once again properly managed. After that the picture becomes a little vague, mainly because we are not too sure of our dates, but it seems that the land survived intact the empty years of the seventh through the ninth centuries A.D., as it had survived the post-Mycenaean dark age, only to fall victim to another case of catastrophic soil erosion when resettlement began in Middle Byzantine times. Careless clearing it must have been, one thinks, that produced the observed result this time.

Two modes of land stabilization can thus be recognized: terracing and, paradoxically, total abandonment. Two modes of destabilization also are observed: overly intensive use, including the clearing of very marginal lands, or a shift to the much less labor-intensive practice of pastoralism. Having arrived at this conclusion for the southern Argolid, we are now waiting with considerable interest to see what the study of other parts of the eastern Mediterranean might tell us. Are we correct in attributing so much to the vagaries of rural economics, or does nature, and especially climate, play a larger role than we have admitted? And if we are correct, do the details fit? Can we indeed read as much from the nature of the deposits about the successes and failures of the Mediterranean farmers as we have been tempted to? Time, and the efforts of others, will tell.

To conclude, we must keep our promise and express an opinion about man's role in the creation of the bare-bones appearance of the landscape of the Argolid in particular and Greece in general. For the southern Argolid that has proved fairly easy to do. Geological studies on land and a geophysical survey at sea, originally designed to find out where the prehistoric shores were and what they might have looked like, have given us the means to estimate fairly accurately how much sediment was eroded from the slopes and deposited in the sea since human beings first began to exploit the landscape. We may restrict our consideration to the last 5,000 years, because there were so few people before then and because there is no evidence at all that they significantly disturbed the landscape. By calculating a redistribution over hills and mountains of all sediment of that age now residing in valleys and on the sea floor, we obtain a layer of soil a good deal less than 1 m thick, far less than what would be needed to clothe the mountains in lush greenery.

But perhaps, one might argue, the southern lands were eroded much more than those in the north, because agriculture was more intensive in the south. Granting this, we recalculate separately for north and south, placing the boundary along the ridge from Koiladha by way of Kranidhi to Ermioni. Less sediment is now to be put back on the mountains in the north, only about 30 cm, and more in the south, just a little over 1 m.

The answer is therefore clear. If ever there was a thick mantle of soil in the Argolid, it was stripped away by the many erosional events of the Ice Age, long before man began to have a hand in the process. Human activity has subsequently contributed to the further removal of soil, but it has not by any means been enough to explain the disappearance of the lush, wooded landscape some imagine to have existed in Classical times. Whether this holds for all of Greece is, of course, another matter, but we are inclined to think that in the main it does.

Chapter 9
•

Growth and Decline: A History of People

A colorful story has unfolded in the previous chapters, rich in variety and nicely balanced, light against dark. Yet an attentive reader will have noticed that, with rare exceptions, we have used only the simplest information. How many sites? How distributed across the landscape? How placed with regard to the soil? We know more, and more can and should be said, in view of the sometimes bewildering complexity of the story. That is best achieved by taking leave of the chronological order that has served us well so far, and shifting to a more topical treatment.

Let us begin by reviewing what we have discovered or surmised about the hierarchy of settlement, the farms, villages, and towns. Numbers of sites and their spread across the land are but the simplest aspect of the survey. More difficult is the question how we are to interpret the sites we have found, how to know what functions they served. Are they the remains of towns, villages, farmhouses, shrines perhaps, or only ancient garbage dumps? Is there really a solid justification for what we have done, for contrasting site patterns of different ages, for trying to make some sense of their changes over time? Or is each pattern wholly unrelated to what went before and came after, so that we are dealing with a classic case of comparing apples and oranges?

If the truth be known, it is far from certain that, except in the Classical towns of Halieis or Hermion, even excavation would definitely establish the function of most of our sites. To some extent that is because archaeological data present such a fragmentary, distorted record of what was once there, all perishables gone, the remainder so often ambiguous in meaning. Moreover, we really know rather little of the simpler facts and artifacts of ancient Greek life, compared with the fine detail found in archaeological studies of Ionian column bases or Mycenaean tombs. It does not help that throughout Greece excavators have neglected those small, inconspicuous sites that form the great majority of our discoveries. In equal measure our uncertainty results from the fact that the functions of most human habitations change while they are being used, even if they are used for only a short time. A farm tower may turn into a fortress, then be converted into an animal pen, and finally become a dumping ground for a neighbor's trash.

Still, for a good many of our sites interpretation is not impossible, as we have illustrated in Chapter 5, and we can improve it by limiting our attempt to identify functions to a simple scheme. Simplest would be a division between settlements—the places where people actually lived—and sites with special purposes such as defense or religion. The criteria on which a division can be based are various: size, artifacts found on the site, architectural remains if there are any, not to mention a dose of common sense. For example, a small site, perhaps less than half a hectare, with a rectangular stone foundation on it and occupied for a single period, is quite likely to have been a farmhouse. That conclusion would be strengthened if we find roof tiles, storage vessels, coarse cooking pots, ceramic lamps, millstones, an oil press perhaps, and, if the farmer was well off, some stucco from his house walls, together with a few pieces of fine pottery. The few farmsteads excavated in Attica do indeed possess all that, and, with due allowance for the changing times, the modern ones are not so different. Yet calling such a site a farmstead is at best an educated guess, and we cannot rule out the possibility that the site might have been used for some totally different purpose. We remain just a little bit uncertain, though not so much that we cannot proceed. Moreover, even if we agree to call it a farmstead, what exactly does that mean? Did a farmer and his family live there the year round, or was it only seasonally occupied by someone whose permanent home was in a nearby city? Were the inhabitants free, or were they perhaps sharecroppers or even slaves?

Special-purpose sites present similar problems. As a group they are defined negatively, by the lack of those characteristics thought to belong to settlements, the absence of any objects indicating that someone lived on them. The identification may be made easier by a few column drums, or a find of bones up-

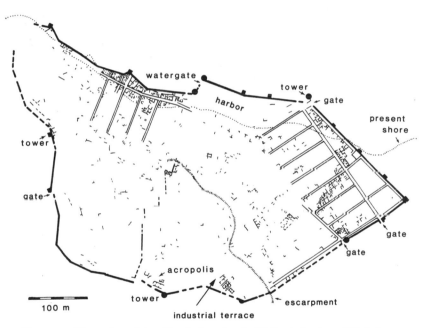

Figure 13. The ruins of the Classical and early Hellenistic city of Halieis can still be seen in the landscape. Part of the city was flooded when the sea rose in the early centuries A.D.; excavation of two temples outside the gates has been carried out by divers. The city possessed an acropolis on a small, steep hill, and a terrace just below it, where industrial activity took place. The residential areas were in the plain near the shore, surrounded completely by a city wall with towers, four land gates, and one watergate. Here and there the city wall is no longer visible (broken lines), and its trace had to be assumed. (After a drawing by Thomas Boyd.)

rooted from a grave, but more often a degree of uncertainty remains here also.

Settlements, too, come in many kinds, from small to large, from a single shepherd's hut to an entire town. A town is vast compared with other sites of its period, and contains a much greater variety of artifacts. It is also, especially since the Archaic period, a likely place to find substantial architectural remains. A Classical or Hellenistic farmhouse, placed in isolation, its remains often including the foundation of a stone tower, is also easy, but the majority of sites of all periods are to us merely "settlements," because doubt remains regarding their place in the scheme of things.

This approach to site functions is minimalist, tentative and definitely conservative, but other scholars may disagree even so with some or all of our interpretations. Nevertheless, rather a surprising amount can be learned from a list of the numbers of sites in each function category for each period (Table 1).

What is most obvious in Table 1 is that towns, and with them urban, or at least proto-urban, life did not appear in the southern Argolid until the seventh century B.C., and that they lost their importance after only a few centuries, not to be resurrected until very recently. The isolated farmstead with its strong tower also became prominent in the later Classical period, but it continued in use longer, until Late Roman days. Settlements with less well defined functions have always been

TABLE I　*Inferred functions of archaeological sites in the southern Argolid*

Period	Town	Farm-stead	Settlement	Shrine	Kiln	Fort	Other
Early Bronze Age			29 (3)				8
Late Bronze Age			21 (4)	(1)		(1)	1
Geometric to Classical	4	10 (1)	86 (5)	7 (2)		(2)	12
Hellenistic to Middle Roman	1	7 (1)	13 (1)	(1)			1
Late Roman	1 (1)	4 (1)	50 (4)	1 (1)	2 (2)		3
Middle Byzantine/ Frankish	1		29 (5)	6 (1)			3

NOTE: Numbers in parentheses are sites of poorly defined age.

the most abundant kind, and during the Bronze Age they were virtually the only ones. There is much variety within this category, ranging from the Early Bronze Age villages to sites so tiny and with finds so few that they could only be assembled in a miscellaneous category labeled as "other."

The picture is enriched if we look at size (Table 2) as well as function. Small sites have always been the most numerous, but as early as 5,000 years ago we find medium-sized (ca. 0.5 ha) and large ones (greater than 1 ha), evidence that differences had already arisen in population and perhaps in function. The Early Bronze Age seems special, because the ratio of small to medium-sized sites is almost 1:1, but that may be mostly because many of the medium-sized sites were reoccupied, so that we cannot be certain of their original dimensions. Even so, rich finds indicate that early in the Bronze Age those were villages rather than farms, and that shortly after the first spread of settlement, about 5,000 years ago, there was already a difference between farms and farm centers. At the opposite end of the range, the smallest sites are not only small indeed, with very few finds, but they are also often found high on scrub-covered limestone ridges. This suggests to us that they were shepherd's huts, sheepfolds, or outlying sheds for tools or produce. Others may have been occupied only seasonally, at planting or harvest time. The simplest sites have just a few flaked stone artifacts, parts of sickles, drills, or simple blades. They probably belong to the Bronze Age, because their distribution resembles that of the other, better-dated sites, but we do not know what they mean, what they were used for, or when precisely they were occupied.

In the Late Bronze Age we see important changes as the proportion of small sites increases considerably. This trend reaches its peak in the fifth and fourth centuries B.C., when by far the largest number of sites appear to be small farms. The evolution goes from a nucleated pattern, with a limited number of villages, to one in which many small sites are dispersed across the landscape with just a few centers, some large enough to be called towns. All over Greece the Archaic period saw the

TABLE 2   Sizes of archaeological sites in the southern Argolid

Period	Small	Medium	Large	Major
Early Bronze Age	13	10	2	
Middle Bronze Age	3		1	
Late Bronze Age	13	3	2	
Geometric	9	3		
Archaic and Classical	28	5	3	2
Classical/Hellenistic	56	14	3	2
Hellenistic to Middle Roman	16	4	2	(1)
Late Roman	31	12	9	(1)
Middle Byzantine/Frankish	27	7	6	(1)

NOTE: Numbers in parentheses are sites of poorly defined age. Small = <0.3 ha; medium = 0.3–1.0 ha; large = 1.0–10.0 ha; major = >10.0 ha.

emergence of towns, often city-states (poleis; sing., polis), which gathered together the functions hitherto performed by a larger number of medium-sized farming centers.

The period from 700 to 300 B.C. also brought the first firmly identified temples, shrines, memorials, cemeteries, wells, and quarries. The appearance of sanctuaries, shrines, and funerary monuments is a phenomenon seen throughout Greece in Late Geometric to early Classical times, and is associated with the rise of the polis. In the southern Argolid, temples were built early (in Archaic times) at Halieis, near Mases on the south slope of the Franchthi promontory, at Hermion, and on the Iliokastro plateau, to mention but a few. To this period also belong cemeteries and funerary monuments at Halieis, Hermion, and Mases. Graves, of course, are an inevitable companion of human settlement. The oldest ones we know of are Neolithic burials in Franchthi cave, but, curiously, graves remain scarce in the southern Argolid until the early historic period, and nothing comparable to the Neolithic cemeteries of Thessaly or the tholos and chamber tombs of Mycenae has been found. One or two stone-lined graves of dubious date and one possible small funerary vase are all we have for the Bronze Age. Yet not only the intensity of our survey precludes the possibility that whole cemeteries have remained undiscovered; we also lack the usual reports from local informants about graves, whether plundered or not. We are somewhat at a loss to explain this, because the Bronze Age in our area, though obviously not so glorious as around Mycenae and Tiryns, seems far from impoverished, but perhaps the population was still truly small. If that is the reason, the greater visibility of graves in the Classical period must indicate a very appreciable rise in the number of people. That conclusion seems to be confirmed by the appearance, at the same time, of many wells and cisterns. Although wells are known elsewhere from the Early Bronze Age on, we have no solid evidence for them in the southern Argolid prior to the Archaic period, and they become common only in Classical times, giving evidence of a greatly increased need for water. Perhaps the climate turned dry in the seventh century B.C., but that is another one of those unprovable hypotheses. It seems more plausible that the population had grown to such a size that springs and streams were no longer sufficient.

This ever increasing diversity in the southern Argolid is the consequence of the emergence during the early historic period of two poleis, or city-states, centered on Halieis and Hermion, both organized in the manner of what economic geographers call a central market system. This pattern can be traced down through the Classical to the Middle Roman period, although the number of sites drops sharply with the later Hellenistic economic depression.

A different pattern appears after the fourth century A.D. In addition to a large number of small sites we see the emergence of many intermediate ones. The pattern is no longer dominated by a few main centers, but by many. Only Hermion seems to have survived with its functions intact. What we see is a combination of two things, a revival of the old village pattern and, something new, the appearance of large agricultural estates, agricultural villas (*villae rusticae*) such as the one excavated at Halieis. These estates, though of very different social structure, functioned much like small villages. A few must also have been industrial centers, because it is at this time that we find large pottery-kiln complexes on small sheltered coves along the shore. The main product of those kilns was storage jars of a characteristic globular shape, probably used to ship the olive oil produced in the area.

The archaeological evidence ends with the Middle Byzantine and Frankish periods, its patterns already resembling the early Modern configuration. The larger sites probably included villages and fortified settlements, perhaps even country manors or monastic holdings, but, so far as we know, Kastri (Ermioni) was the only town in the region. We base this conclusion on clusters of small settlements and chapels in its vicinity, but little else is known about this period.

To a first approximation, the geographic history of the area can thus be reduced to two alternating modes. One, the first to appear, is based on villages, of which there were many scattered across the landscape, each serving a cluster of farm sites. The other we are tempted to call urban; it evolved by gathering the functions and at least some of the population of several smaller centers into one or more towns, while villages and numerous farms were dispersed to the far corners of the landscape. Having begun in the Archaic period, the urban pattern lasted for several centuries, until its gradual dissolution in Hellenistic and Roman times.

Let us next turn from this discussion of the functions of individual sites to a consideration of the function of the entire southern Argolid within a larger economic and political sphere. As we have seen in previous chapters, various economic and political forces have played a part in the history of the southern Argolid, causing the settlement patterns from late in the Neolithic onward to oscillate between one consisting of a few widely spaced sites and another of many and inevitably closely spaced ones. We shall call the first pattern *nucleated* and the second *dispersed*. This alternation of nucleation and dispersion will be our next theme.

That nucleated and dispersed settlement patterns have alternated throughout the history of Greece is not a new discovery. It has been thoroughly discussed by J. M. Wagstaff, Colin Renfrew, and John Cherry in a study of the island of Melos that precedes and parallels ours, as well as by Anthony Snodgrass and John Bintliff in connection with their Boeotia survey. Wagstaff and his colleagues concluded, as we have done, that external economic and social forces determined which of the two modes prevailed on the island at any given time. The key factor can be summed up in a single word: exploitation. When some greater outside power had control over Melos, a nucleated pattern prevailed, whereas a dispersed one can be seen when Melos was master of its own economic destiny. Nucleated coastal settlements served as an effective means for external control over the resources of the island. When, on the other hand, the island was economically independent, the inhabitants found it more convenient to live near the scattered patches of agricultural land that fed them.

There are parallels between the history of Melos and that of the southern Argolid, especially during the drastic economic contractions of the Middle Bronze Age and of later Hellenistic times, but the differences are equally striking. For most of its history, the settlements of the southern Argolid were dispersed, even during times of outward economic orientation and prosperity. Melos, in contrast, presented the opposite pattern when outside influences were dominant.

The investigators of Melos wisely refrained from indicating whether the external influence in Melos was chiefly economic or political. In the southern Argolid, on the other hand, we know that during Classical and early Hellenistic times the dominant influence was economic rather than political, an opportunity for the area to interact with and profit from external markets. We are inclined to assume that the same was true for earlier and later periods of prosperity, which were also accompanied by dispersed settlement patterns.

It therefore seems that there were subtle differences in the impact of external forces, political ones on Melos on the one hand, economic ones in the southern Argolid on the other. To phrase it a little more precisely: in the case of Melos an external power exploited the island's resources to its own benefit, whereas in the Argolid it was the area itself that used its resources to exploit the profitable markets of a wider world. The only time when that was demonstrably not true in the Argolid was during the eighteenth and early nineteenth centuries A.D. At that time, the production of the area was siphoned off through ecclesiastic and secular agricultural estates for the benefit of commercial establishments on the offshore islands. A similar situation may have existed in the later Middle Ages, or even earlier, but we cannot be certain of that. The differences in settlement history between Melos and the southern Argolid are perhaps due to geographic circumstances. Melos is smaller than our area and even farther away from the economic centers of the mainland, and it has only one harbor, in contrast to the three of the southern Argolid. Perhaps there is some threshold in size or in position relative to larger polities that is significant in the history of settlement and that we cannot yet consider because of our lack of data.

For a justification of our hypothesis we look to the present. There is no doubt that Melos today is typical for rural Greece and the Argolid is not. As is true virtually everywhere else, Melian settlements are diminishing in number, and the population is dwindling even in the few remaining nucleated villages and towns. Nearly everywhere in Greece population has been lost to Athens, and entire communities have been abandoned or combined into nucleated settlements better suited to serve as gateways between the agricultural hinterland and the market of greater Athens.

The recent history of the southern Argolid is just the opposite, as we have said earlier, in Chapters 1 and 7. The growth of Athens has provided a large, convenient, and secure market that anyone can take advantage of without leaving the area, no matter what his preferred economic activity, boat building, tomato growing, the tourist trade, or olive culture. It is not Athens that exploits the Argolid; instead, the southern Argolid exploits, by choice and with much success, the opportunities offered by its large northern neighbor.

Obviously, the terms nucleated and dispersed are at best sweeping generalizations, whose use does not fully correspond to reality. No matter how convenient polar opposites are in any argument, more often than not the observed pattern is in some sense transitional between the two. Site size, site function, and the whole complex of local and regional economic and political forces now and in the past should all be elements in our interpretation, with the result that the picture would become more realistic but also inevitably less clear. It is quite likely, for example, that the large Late Roman estates were not always locally owned and that, when exploited for the benefit of an external landlord, they created a situation more like the Melian and less like what we believe to be true for the Argolid during the Classical and early Hellenistic periods.

Let us shy away from such complexities, and raise instead the question what the local, internal economic reasons may have been for the two contrasting settlement patterns. What were the land use practices that corresponded to those feast and famine modes of existence? Nucleated settlements, especially in the Early Bronze Age, seem to correspond to grain agriculture mainly for the farmer's own needs, perhaps assisted by pastoralism. They are invariably found near the best soils, though leaving as much good land as possible free to grow crops. The distance a farmer must walk to and from his fields is thus minimized, and the bulky grain need not be transported far to the place where it will be consumed. More distant lands are given over to sheep and goats.

The production of olive oil, on the other hand, is best served by a more dispersed mode of living. Olive trees, unlike grain, demand attention at various times throughout the year, and it is much more efficient to press the oil right beneath the trees than to transport the fruit back to the village. The required investment in capital goods can be large, and the olive presses and storage jars, as well as temporary housing for the workers, are best placed near the groves. Grain, obviously, is needed in even greater amounts for a labor force that itself needs to be increased to tend the trees. That puts pressure on the best land, and growing grain among the trees becomes worthwhile even though the yield may be relatively low. Olive trees are more tolerant of poor soil and little water than cereals; consequently we find their groves mainly on marginal lands far from the original villages, with the dispersed sites for their exploitation nearby. Inevitably, therefore, the cost increases, but because extensive olive culture beyond the small needs of the farmers themselves is always done for sale in external markets, this does not matter. When the times turn bad, one can always retrench, abandon the outlying fields to the shepherd, and once again settle in nucleated centers near the best land until the economy improves.

What we are saying, then, is that the nucleated and dispersed settlement patterns correspond in a first approximation to grain agriculture (with some pastoralism) and olive arboriculture (or other diversified cash agriculture). The dispersed pattern is the more expensive of the two and can only exist when external demand justifies the increased production. We should immediately add, however, that the Early Bronze Age settlement pattern too might be called dispersed, although not to the degree seen in the Classical, early Hellenistic, or Late Roman times. Yet the evidence for extensive culture of the olive during the Bronze Age is limited, and we do not believe that it was then a significant element in the rural economy. Obviously, the reasoning given above should not be too confidently applied to any and all conditions; there are likely to be factors involved that we have not examined.

The Argolid is too dry, its soils too poor, to support easily on its own more than a modest number of people, and the labor necessary to wring a surplus in oil or wool from the land is too great to undertake unless the incentive is strong. On the other hand, trade with the outside world seems to have had its beginnings in the Neolithic or perhaps even earlier, and was therefore an ancient tradition for this region. In the Bronze Age, this tradition may have taken on a new meaning when, for the first time, centers of population and sources of power developed at the periphery of the southern Argolid, namely, on some of the islands and in the plain of Argos. We do not think it coincidental that the first dispersions of settlement occurred in the third and again in the second millennium B.C., at the same time that in the Aegean the first proto-urban centers emerged, with needs that the inhabitants of our area may have hurried to satisfy. Consequently, a habit of responding to outside economic forces may have been established early, continuing to the present day to fluctuate with the ebb and flow of those forces. The southern Argolid has never been a center of political or economic power; indeed, it is an insignificant part of Greece. Yet, in its vicissitudes it serves as an index, a barometer, to measure the state of affairs in a larger world, growing as it did in times of prosperity and security, and wasting away when the fortunes of the surrounding states declined. The present time is only one more example of this, helpful because it gives us the details that are irretrievable from the more distant past.

As in the rest of Greece, the history of settlement in the southern Argolid is not one of smooth progress from simple, primitive beginnings to a complex and superior present. Growth alternated with stability, both punctuated with occasional and at times sudden bursts of change. This history is powered by a vast array of forces, ranging from natural ones, such as climate or the capacity of the soil to adjust to exploitation, to the internal and external political and economic drives we have just discussed. Whenever possible, the people of the Ermionis have reached out to exploit their land and water to the utmost, and have so achieved prosperity. At other times they overextended themselves; precariously dependent on the outside world, they were often forced to abandon their lands, or were wiped out completely by a sudden change of fortune.

We have said little about the important problem of population history so far; though it is a difficult one, it must be dealt with. Sites, of course, were once inhabited by people, but it would be a serious mistake to assume that more sites invariably mean more people, or their abandonment a decreasing population. In our western European and North American experience populations rise continuously, inexorably, and, in the eyes of many, ominously. That is not, however, how the population history of Greece has been. During the Turkish domination, from the fifteenth to the nineteenth century, the few

European visitors found a land that was, with a few major exceptions, depopulated, a few impoverished peasants living among the ruins of earlier, greater times. Most observers agreed that in the eighteenth and the early nineteenth century the population of Greece was still far below what it had been in the remote past. Such depopulation was not, of course, unique to Greece. Beginning in the fourteenth century, the Black Plague decimated Europe several times. Its effect has not been recorded for Greece but cannot be doubted. Unfortunately, we can only guess at Greek population statistics prior to the nineteenth century; they are vanishingly rare because the archives of the Byzantine Empire were lost when Constantinople was sacked in 1204 and again in 1453 A.D., and those of its Ottoman successor are little known in the West. Farther back, for Roman or Classical times, data are rare.

Still, we should try to reconstruct the population history in our area, because without it our settlement patterns are lifeless fossil bones, with nothing remaining of the flesh that once adhered to them. In the end, archaeology today is interested in people rather than things, remote as that goal sometimes seems, and so far we have failed to take this final account of the people themselves. For better or for worse (and it cannot be very good) we should try.

Only with the greatest reservations might one measure the population directly from the archaeological remains. It is obvious that many people can be packed into just a handful of large settlements, whereas a few individualists may each occupy one of a large number of scattered small sites. Changes in the number of settlements are therefore not meaningful unless we take into consideration what kinds of settlements they might have been, which is itself, as we have seen earlier, not a simple question. Extrapolations from periods of known population must come to our aid, and we might also employ a theoretical argument or two.

Paradoxically, the earliest times are not the most difficult. A century of ethnographic studies of hunters and gatherers from around the world has shown that small bands of people, usu-

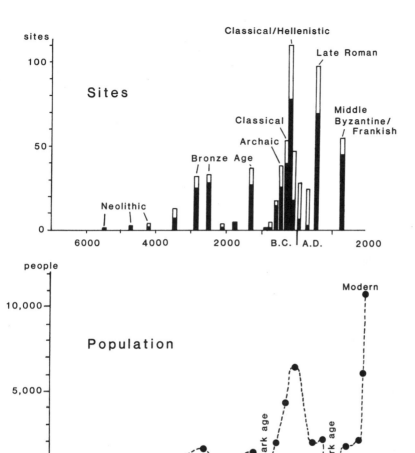

Figure 14. These graphs compare the variation in number of sites over time in the southern Argolid (top) with our estimates of the changes in population (bottom). The rapid growth in the Bronze Age, and again during the Classical and Classical/Hellenistic, Late Roman, and Middle Byzantine periods, is obvious, as are the two dark ages, during which the population sharply decreased or even virtually disappeared. In a broad sense the two graphs are similar, showing ups and downs at the same times in the past. In detail, however, there are important differences: compare, for example, the very similar Classical/Hellenistic and Late Roman site numbers with the strikingly different population estimates. Note that we have included the modern population, the first to exceed the Classical/Hellenistic one in number.

ally numbering 25 to 50 men, women, and children, must be supported by large tracts of land. How many people and how large a tract depend, of course, on the climate, the vegetation, the wildlife, and many other factors. Estimates vary, because only in marginal environments have modern representatives been left more or less to themselves, whereas conditions were by no means so poor in the past. A band of 25 to 50 Hadza, living in Tanzania in a setting somewhat similar to that of the Argolid steppe during a glacial interval, requires from 175 to 350 km² to make a living. The southern Argolid, even when the sea was low and the coastal plains wide, was never larger than that. It is unlikely that more than 25 persons, or at most 50, could have fed themselves there at any time during the Palaeolithic, and the whole of the present Argolid might have supported fewer than 300.

We think that this level was hardly exceeded even in early postglacial times, notwithstanding the warmer climate, greater rainfall, or consumption of big fish. The single small settlement at Franchthi bears that out. With the introduction of a food-producing economy of grain, sheep, and goats, the environmental limits were gradually relaxed, but throughout the Neolithic there is still no evidence for more than one small village. Though estimates of the population of primitive agricultural villages are as much guesswork as those for hunter-gatherers, not many would object to a maximum of 100 persons per hectare of village area. That, the most generous estimate possible, would accord the Franchthi village in and outside the cave from 100 to 400 people, and we would favor the lower number. Not very many indeed, but it seems to have been the whole population of our area for almost 3,000 years.

Expansion began in the very latest Neolithic, and by the middle of the third millennium B.C. there were four or five hamlets or small villages in the area, in addition to many small sites that may have been farms. The largest of those Early Bronze Age villages was near Fournoi; it has yielded the remains of twenty different domestic hearths, one per dwelling, we suppose. Another nine or ten localities found in adjoining fields were probably part of the same settlement. Taking five people as a convenient hearth-multiplier, we estimate 150 inhabitants at Fournoi, or 750 for all five villages. One notes that, with artifacts scattered over four or perhaps slightly more hectares, this number could be somewhat greater. Villages at Ayios Kosmas, in Attica, and at Lerna, in the plain of Argos, both from 1.0 to 1.5 ha in area, may have had similar populations of 100 to 240, depending on how many people were packed into them. Our villages would have been very little different from these. Adding the other sites in our area as worth a family or two each, we can push the population of the whole southern Argolid to around 1,200 people. That number, endowed with an uncertainty of at least 20 percent, and equal to one-tenth of the present population, seems reasonable, and gives us a kind of scale for later prehistoric and historic times.

Between the end of the Early Bronze Age and the Mycenaean period we see a pattern of extreme nucleation, but the few remaining sites are small. There must have been a drop in population as well, rather than merely a concentration of the many in fewer places. In the Late Bronze Age, many new sites were founded, until once more we have about five villages and a swarm of smaller sites consisting of hamlets and farms. Much like the Early Bronze Age it was, and the population probably climbed back to the previous level also. Then, toward the end of the thirteenth century B.C., there begins a period for which, except for a handful of sherds on the peak of what may have been a fortified hill, we have little evidence of habitation for about a century, and then nothing at all. It was an unsettled time for the whole of the eastern Mediterranean, and, whatever the cause, we are justified in concluding that, apart from the occasional shepherd or sailor, no one lived in the southern Argolid until the middle of the tenth century B.C., or even somewhat later.

Argolid population history becomes complex in the following Greek, Roman, and medieval periods, but we seem to be on somewhat firmer ground nevertheless. Settlers, perhaps pastoralists looking for farmland, arrived from the Argive plain, Lakonia, and Attica. Halieis, Hermion, Mases, and Eileoi had been established by the seventh century B.C., their rise indicating a population larger than at any time in the Bronze Age. Norman Pounds, a historical geographer from Indiana University, has used a variety of archaeological and historical data, and calculations of the amount of arable land needed to feed city dwellers, to give us the means to estimate the population of our cities. In addition, we know from excavations that some 450 or 500 houses occupied the 18 ha within the walls of Halieis. Using our hearth multiplier of five persons, this gives us 2,500 people for the whole town, and that fits well with what Pounds would have guessed, namely 2,700.

Hermion may have been a little larger, but Mases was definitely a good deal smaller than Halieis, probably no more than one-fifth its size, and so the three main towns together accounted for about 6,500 people. In addition, we know of at least five villages with, shall we say, 100 per village, and some 70 farms with a few permanent inhabitants each. One does not want to carry such calculations too far, but 6,800 to 7,300 people in the entire southern Argolid seems a fair enough estimate. Of course, many of the small sites may have merely been seasonal shelters for people who had their main residence in the towns; that would reduce the total by a small amount. Obviously, in terms of the population the big increase since the Bronze Age came in the towns; in the countryside the population during early historic times may not have been all that different.

Unfortunately, this time of prosperity and population growth did not last much past the brief lifetime of Alexander the Great. In the decades following his death many sites in the Argolid were abandoned, including Halieis and all of its suburban settlements, leaving only a few around Hermion. Inevitably, this implies a loss of population, and up to the Late Roman period the area was thinly settled, with most people living in or near Hermion, the only town. It is impossible to say how many remained, but they were surely far fewer than half the number that lived there in the Classical period, and probably less even than that.

The decline had reversed by the fourth century A.D. In the years following the foundation of Constantinople, the region experienced growth and, apparently, peaceful conditions, because, so far as we know, the many settlements were entirely without fortifications. We have already noted that some of them were large estates, like the one excavated at Halieis, privately owned enterprises where serfs (*coloni*) worked for absentee landlords to produce, among other things, olive oil for export. How many people lived on those estates? Our estimate hovers around 100 each, or a little less; together with perhaps as many as 2,000 in Hermion, which had a church and a basilica and therefore was a town of some consequence, that makes about 2,800 to 3,000 people for the whole area. Given the large number of sites at this time, the second largest in all history until the nineteenth century, that is a surprisingly small number. It clearly illustrates how numbers of sites by themselves are not enough for estimating population densities.

The Late Roman prosperity ended in the seventh century A.D., the last sites disappeared, though perhaps not all at the same time, and the area remained virtually empty for at least 200 years. Only with the renaissance of the Middle Byzantine period, sometime during the ninth or tenth century A.D., were hearth fires once more kindled in the Ermionis, tentatively at first, in farms nestling near chapels high in the valleys and out of sight of the sea. At Kastri (Ermioni), the ancient city wall was refurbished, and it is safe to assume that the town regained its position as the principal settlement. Shortly afterward, by 1288 A.D., Kranidhi was founded, probably by the conjoining of several smaller villages. Our archaeological and historical data are imperfect for this and the following period, but one may guess that the population was perhaps halfway between that of the Early Bronze Age and that of Late Roman times. For a much later time, figures given by travelers or derived from the eighteenth century cadastral surveys of the Venetians have allowed Peter Topping to estimate the population of Messenia, in the southwestern Peloponnese, and of the Peloponnese as a whole for the late seventeenth and early eighteenth centuries. If we judiciously scale those estimates to the southern Argolid we get a number of 1,500 to 2,000, which fits well for the small towns of Kastri and Kranidhi, five or six villages, and the usual scatter of hamlets and farms.

Thus between the sack of Constantinople in 1204 and the Greek War of Independence the population fluctuated around this figure through war, conquest, disease, and brief periods of tranquility. Then, after independence was achieved in 1832, our information improves greatly, and we see two large increases. The first, to nearly 7,000, came almost immediately as peace, the commerce of the offshore islands Idhra, Spetsai, and Poros, and the citizens of the new national capital at Navplion, later at Athens, brought economic opportunities to the farmers, herders, fishermen, and sailors of the Argolid. By 1851 there were about 10,000 inhabitants, and around the turn of the century some 12,000 people made their homes in the area. After a minor setback during the Great Depression of the 1930's and World War II, the population rose again; new settlements have been founded, and old ones have grown. Today there live in the area a little more than 12,000 people, an all-time high, but one sure to diminish once again as the pendulum swings, and the outside world has fewer opportunities to offer.

Epilogue

•

What Next?

The question with which we begin this final discourse can be taken in two senses: What should we do next in the ongoing study of the southern Argolid? And what is in store in the future for the people of the Argolid themselves? The main features of our conclusions should by now be familiar. The southern Argolid, peaceful and even sleepy as it appears, has witnessed repeated upheavals both natural and cultural. The sea has changed its level by more than 100 m over the last 100,000 years, thereby greatly altering the shape of the peninsula, while on land we detected no fewer than seven episodes of erosion and alluviation, destructive to slopes and valley floors alike. Three of those belong in the Ice Age, but four came within the last 5,000 years or so, and we see in them the hand of man.

The towns and villages that one now finds in the area have also proven changeable in time and space. Our findings show that variation has been the rule, with settlement expanding and contracting for thousands of years. In the last 8,000 years no fewer than five peaks in the number of sites and their degree of dispersion occurred even before the modern era, with at least four intervening periods when settlement was severely limited or virtually absent. We have linked the last four events of soil erosion and alluviation to this shifting pattern of settlement rather than to climatic or other agents, arguing that agricultural practices, the overuse, underuse, or complete abandonment of the land, were the principal causes of alluviation or stability.

Cultural factors have been invoked also to explain the dynamics of the settlement pattern. Owing to its size and to its location on the seaways between the Peloponnese, central Greece, and the islands, the Ermionis throughout the last 5,000 years or more has relied upon external markets in times of prosperity and occasionally also for its survival. The scattered and uneven distribution of arable land has meant that during times of economic growth settlements were forced to disperse, often to remote locations. On the other hand, when the Argolid went through the inevitable times of depression and contraction, a retrenchment of settlements was the response to economic and military upheavals in the larger Greek world.

With this book we have attempted to sketch the prehistory and history of the southern Argolid, impressionistic in its broad outline as a Chinese ink painting. This design runs somewhat counter to the everyday course of archaeological and geological study, which concentrates upon particularistic and often highly specialized research. The traditional image of archaeologists and geologists, whose disciplines evolved together in the nineteenth century, is one of scientists roaming the countryside picking up rocks or artifacts and examining them intently, their eyes rarely lifted to the wide panorama in front. Today that image may have come to include persons immobilized in front of a computer screen, as we are at this moment, or hunched over objects laid out on a laboratory table. The image is true to life: the everyday concern of the scientist is with detail, and that is the reality most likely to command his attention. The survey archaeologist in the field finds a tiny fragment of stone or pottery on a site, something wholly without apparent interest, but to the specialist the shape of the stone or the traces of painted decoration on the potsherd have considerable meaning. They may be known, after many excavations and decades of scholarship, to belong to particular phases of the past; perhaps they can be dated to very specific times, say the fourth century B.C. The insignificant trace of black paint on that tiny scrap of burnt clay thus tells the archaeologist when its site was occupied, and sometimes a good deal more. It is not the search for such specific facts that sends him out into the field, however, not this little detail by itself, but the opportunity ahead to think of what it might mean if joined to other, equally small elements. Are there other sites dated to the same period? What were those people doing way out here? The list could be expanded infinitely. Inevitably, thousands of such facts, the wealth of observations gathered in years of searching, sorting, measuring, analyzing and classifying artifacts and other observations, must come before anything like a big picture will emerge.

We have taken the rare step of attempting to outline the big picture for the southern Argolid while part of the study of our material by teams of specialists is still in progress. Our own tentative conclusions, having taken shape over the years as a result of our personal analysis of the data, solitary meditation, and innumerable dinner table conversations, have matured to a point at which they appear sufficient for exposure to more general scrutiny. Study continues, however, and we must expect to see many changes in the details, and perhaps even in some of the larger features of the conclusions we have presented here.

This is the inexorable course of research: each scholar eventually reaches a stage at which, in full awareness of his shortcomings, the formulation and publication of his thought become the next logical step, needed to stimulate his colleagues to examine and evaluate it, to reinterpret the patterns he has perceived, to gather new data and, with fresh minds, correct and elaborate his conclusions and put forward new ones. The full publication of the excavations at Franchthi cave and Halieis will surely change our views on the Stone Age and on the later Classical period, because no amount of surface reconnaissance can provide the wealth of detail that is yielded by an excavation. In some sense, our survey has been analogous to one more excavation in the region: instead of concentrating upon the study of a single site tested by carefully placed trenches, we have tested the whole of the region by equally carefully chosen mapping transects. Our final results are thus one more contribution to the archaeological and environmental picture; they not only depend upon our co-workers, who are sifting through historical records, ethnographic notes, and the piles of potsherds, stone tools, and other debris we collected, but will stimulate them as well.

Already now we are able to raise many a question, unanswerable at the moment, but likely to loom large in the future. Have we, for example, overestimated the novel aspects of the Neolithic? Were its culture and technology perhaps partly or entirely indigenous? Can trade and exchange have been so important at any time as we have assumed? Were the later Classical farmsteads really producing olive oil for more than local consumption? Have we failed to appreciate fully the role of fishing in the local economy throughout the past? The questions proliferate, even though the answers remain elusive.

Now to the other side of our question: What is in store for the people of the southern Argolid? Our prognosis is not comforting. The current prosperity is proclaimed by the new hotels, the countless cars, houses, TV antennas, smart fashions, and all the other appurtenances of the modern industrial economy in evidence everywhere. The vital signs are good: growing population, decline in infant mortality, increasing per capita income, new schools, new roads, and soon, we hope, even an archaeological museum. So why our disquiet? For one thing, the water table is being dangerously drawn down, while agricultural production has been pushed to every corner of the landscape, creating a precarious balance between maintenance and erosion. For another, the economy has evolved to the point of absolute dependence upon the outside world. The agriculture is designed to provide Athens and even the European Common Market with olive oil, fruit, and vegetables; most incomes depend on this, or on tourism, the service industry, the merchant marine, or emigration and remittances from overseas. A crystal ball is hardly needed to see what havoc war or a worldwide economic crisis might wreak. The Argolid is doomed, in our view, to swing once again into obscurity and poverty, only to return to prosperity in some still unforesee- able future, when the water supply has been replenished by the sparse winter rains, and the sediments from the slopes have settled in the valleys, so that once more the long march onward may begin.

Reference Material

Glossary

alluvium. Sediments deposited in stream valleys and on coastal plains by rivers. They range from boulders and gravels to sand and loam, and include debris flows.

debris flow. A usually fast, sudden flow of mud, boulders, sand, and water resulting from a catastrophic, sheetwise erosion of soil on valley slopes. It devastates the fields on the valley floor and leaves behind an extensive layer of mixed boulders, sand, and loam.

dispersed. Settlement pattern in which many sites are scattered across the landscape. The term does not say anything about the size of the sites, nor about whether they come in a hierarchy of sizes or functions. Compare *nucleated.*

hunter-gatherers. People who live by hunting, fishing, shellfish collecting, and the gathering of wild greens, fruit, and nuts. They do not depend on crops or on domesticated animals. Modern examples are the Bushmen of the Kalahari in South Africa, or some bands of aborigines in the interior Australian desert.

maquis. The main natural vegetation of rocky or stony Greek mountainsides. It is dominated by shrubs such as junipers and prickly oak, and has many aromatic plants typical for the low vegetation of Mediterranean hills.

nucleated. Settlement pattern in which the landscape contains only a few widely spaced sites. Like its contrasted term, dispersed, the word nucleated says nothing about either the size or the function of the sites that make up the pattern.

ophiolite. Dark volcanic rock usually associated with the deep ocean floor. It weathers easily and deeply and produces a soil rich in calcium and magnesium. Various rock types are included under this term, such as basalt and serpentinite. In the southern Argolid, the weathered ophiolite produces some of the most fertile soils.

pastoralism. Practice of herding sheep and goats for a living (or cattle, for that matter, in regions other than the Argolid). See also *transhumance*.

phrygana. First vegetation type to colonize abandoned land; also common on very stony slopes with little soil. It is rich in spectacular spring flowers, and is thought to evolve at times into maquis.

polis (pl. *poleis*). The ancient Greeks' name for their principal political unit, the independent city-state, usually consisting of a town and its territory.

subsistence agriculture. The provision of crops exclusively or primarily for the farmer's own use, as contrasted with the growing of cash crops for sale. In Greece in ancient times, and to some extent still today, wheat and such staples as beans or lentils were grown as a subsistence crop; olives and grapes, on the other hand, for both home use and sale.

transhumance. The practice of herding sheep and goats in one area in the winter, and in a different, distant one in summer. The practice often involves long seasonal migrations of flocks, herders, and some members of their families. Transhumants in the Argolid, for example, until very recently grazed their flocks in the summer in the highlands of the central Peloponnese, then brought them back to the southern Argolid for winter grazing in lowland fields and olive orchards.

villa rustica (pl. *villae rusticae*). A large Roman farm, to a high degree self-sufficient and functioning like a small village. Though owned by a landlord, most *villae rusticae* were worked by serfs and were largely self-contained, with housing for the overseer and work force, and the farm industry necessary for a large scale operation.

Bibliographic Essay

A GUIDE FOR GENERAL READING

Books on ancient Greece are in ample supply, but in this section we limit our choice to those that provide a general introduction to the topics we have covered and to those that expand their scope. As a general introduction to the early history of Greece, one might consult Anthony Andrewes, *Greek Society* (Harmondsworth, 1971), and, for an overview of daily life, Chester G. Starr's popular book, *The Ancient Greeks* (Oxford, 1974). M. I. Finley, *Early Greece: The Bronze and Archaic Ages* (New York, 1970), provides an introduction in the emergence of culture, and Emily Vermeule wrote a charming book, though somewhat heavy on detail for a first overview and now a little out of date, *Greece in the Bronze Age* (Chicago, 1964).

As a traveler in Greece, though perhaps only on paper, no one should miss the words of Pausanias, ably translated for the Penguin Classics by Peter Levi (Harmondsworth, 1984); they are a pleasure to read even today.

Many special subjects deserve attention even if we keep away from traditional subjects such as ancient Greek art, architecture, and literature. The wave of Greek colonization after the dark age is of interest in the context of this book, and John Boardman's *The Greeks Overseas* (London, 1982), is comprehensive and beautifully illustrated. On ancient economics there is little that is not heavily burdened with jargon or very technical, but M. I. Finley's *Economy and Society in Ancient Greece* (Harmondsworth, 1981) and *The Ancient Economy* (Berkeley and Los Angeles, 1973) go some way to fill the gap, while Finley's style is a pleasure to read. Anthony Snodgrass's *Archaic Greece: The Age of Experiment* (Berkeley and Los Angeles, 1980) offers a thought-provoking view of Greece in the age of the first city-states.

Surprisingly, there is very little on the Byzantine story outside the scholarly literature; one might, if provoked, try Speros Vryonis, *Byzantium and Europe* (New York, 1967). On the other hand, many are the books on Mycenae, and they are easy to find; one that deals with the palace economy as it is reflected in the Linear B inscriptions is John Chadwick's *The Mycenaean World* (Cambridge, 1977). Another is Lord William Taylour's *The Mycenaeans* (London, 1983).

On modern rural Greece there is quite a lot, and we must choose. Ernestine Friedl has described life in a small Greek village in Boeotia in *Vasilika, A Village in Modern Greece* (New York, 1965), and J. K. Campbell deals with the wandering shepherd families of recent times, the Sarakatsani, in *Honour, Family, and Patronage* (Oxford, 1974). C. M. Woodhouse's *Modern Greece: A Short History* (London, 1977) is a good, readable introduction to the fascinating history of modern Greece. We also like Arnold Toynbee's *The Greeks and Their Heritages* (Oxford, 1981), a look at Greek perceptions of themselves over the course of a long history.

For the southern Argolid, pickings are thus far slim, and not so easily found. In 1976, Michael Jameson collected a set of popular articles on the Argolid in a single issue of the magazine *Expedition*, published by the University Museum of the University of Pennsylvania (vol. 19, no. 1). A more formal collection, with Jameson's own paper on the Akte as well as others on traditional farming, on the "thousand year road" of the shepherds, and on olive culture, is included in *Regional Variation in Modern Greece and Cyprus: Toward a Perspective on the Ethnography of Greece*, edited by M. Dimen and E. Friedl (Annals of the New York Academy of Sciences, vol. 268: New York, 1976). Soon also there will be available a substantial volume of new historical and ethnographic studies of the Argolid in *Shepherds, Farmers, and Sailors: Economy and Regional Development in the Argolid Peninsula* (Stanford University Press, forthcoming), edited by Susan B. Sutton.

DOCUMENTATION AND REFERENCING

Preface and Introduction

As stated in the Preface, this book is intended for a wide, mainly nonprofessional audience interested in Greece and in its role in the history of civilization. To serve that audience best, we dispensed in the text with the usual elaborate footnotes and frequent references to the literature, reserving such documentary material for a separate section at the end, where it would not interrupt the flow of the discourse. Here, then, is a selection of references that provide further illumination, proof, counterarguments, and the background of supportive or contrary opinion on which the text rests. Though by no means complete, the listing should be useful to those readers who require greater depth. A more comprehensive bibliography will eventually be presented in the main publication of the Argolid survey (Jameson et al., forthcoming). We note that so far only preliminary reports exist for the excavations in the area, viz., for Halieis, Boyd and Rudolph (1978), Jameson (1969, 1974), and Rudolph (1979, 1984), and, for the Franchthi cave, Jacobsen (1969, 1973a, 1973b, 1976, 1981). Definitive excavation reports are now beginning to appear for Franchthi, e.g., Hansen (forthcoming), Jacobsen (forthcoming), Perlès (forthcoming), and van Andel and Sutton (forthcoming). The views of Classical Greek authors on forests and deforestations have been presented by Hughes (1983), Meiggs (1982), and Rackham (1983). A summary of surveys accomplished and in progress in Greece can be found in Keller and Rupp (1983). The relation between settlement patterns, land use, and soil erosion has been discussed in detail by van Andel et al. (1986). More general studies on prehistoric land use and its impact on the landscape are by Bell (1982) and Butzer (1974, 1982).

Chapter 1   A Greek Countryside

Jameson (1976) provides an overview of the geography, rural economy, and history of the Argolid as an introduction to a series of papers dealing with the modern anthropology of the region (Clark-Forbes, 1976; Forbes and Koster, 1976; Gavrielides, 1976; Koster and Koster, 1976). More recent are Forbes (1982) and Murray and Kardulias (1986), and shortly also Sutton (forthcoming). The geography and climate are described in NID (1944). A series of brief but illuminating articles on modern anthropology and archaeology in the Argolid can be found in the magazine *Expedition*, volume 19, number 1 (1976), published by the University Museum of the University of Pennsylvania, and in Dimen and Friedl (1976).

As concerns the environments of the southern Argolid past and present, we refer to Hansen (1980, and forthcoming), Sheehan (1979), and Sheehan and Whitehead (1981) for the paleobotany; to Bachmann and Risch (1978, 1979), Bannert and Bender (1968), Süsskoch (1967), and Vrielinck (1982) for the geology; to Pope and van Andel (1984) and van Andel and Sutton (forthcoming) for the late Quaternary history of erosion and alluviation; to Flemming (1968) and van Andel and Lianos (1983, 1984) for changes in sea level and the position of the shoreline; and to Shackleton and van Andel (1986) for the history of shore environments and their resources.

Chapter 2   Walking in the Fields: Archaeology Without Digging

The archaeological survey of the southern Argolid and its objectives were laid out in detail by Jameson (1976); a brief description of the survey during the years 1979–81 is given by Runnels (1983a), and a more comprehensive one by Runnels and van Andel (1987). Other works of interest include the study of modern sites, archaeological sites in the making, by Murray and Kardulias (1986). Full publication of the artifacts found during our survey is being prepared in a volume edited by Mark H. Munn, Daniel J. Pullen, and Curtis N. Runnels.

Accounts of early scientific surveys and their procedures and results can be found in McDonald and Rapp (1972) and Hope Simpson (1981). The full range of modern survey work in Greece can be appreciated by scanning the many entries in Keller and Rupp (1983) and Dyson (1982), and by looking at the detailed publications of the surveys of Melos (Wagstaff and Cherry, 1982), Boeotia (Bintliff and Snodgrass, 1985), and Messenia (McDonald and Rapp, 1972), which are similar to the Argolid project.

Chapter 3   Hunting the Wild Ass: Earliest Man in the Southern Argolid

The present Mediterranean climate has been summarized by Perry (1981), Tollner (1976), and Wigley and Farmer (1982), but little is known regarding the glacial climate and its transition to present conditions (Lamb, 1982). Here the information comes mainly from pollen data in northern Greece, thoroughly summarized by van Zeist and Bottema (1982); additional information on a more global basis is given by Peterson et al. (1979). For the southern Argolid itself, conditions have to be inferred from paleobotanical data (Hansen, 1980, and forthcoming) and by comparison with central Greece (e.g., Bottema, 1979). The landscape was much different at lower sea level (van Andel and Shackleton, 1982; van Andel and Lianos, 1983), with large coastal plains, but the fauna of those plains and of the inland areas is only imperfectly known from preliminary reports on the excavations in Franchthi cave (Payne, 1975, 1982, 1985). Marine resource use does not become important in the area until the Mesolithic (Shackleton, in press; Shackleton and van Andel, 1980, 1986).

The earliest dated find in Greece is the famous skull from Petralona, in Chalkidhiki, in northern Greece, but the dating of the find and its context remain controversial (Stringer et al., 1979; Wintle and Jacobs, 1982; Poulianos, 1981). It is clearly, however, one of the earliest representatives of our species yet known. The sparse finds from this period in the southern Argolid have been discussed by Bialor and Jameson (1962) and Pope et al. (1984). The discussion of the Franchthi cave Palaeolithic rests on the excavation reports of Jacobsen (1969, 1973a, 1973b, 1979). See also Perlès (forthcoming) and Jacobsen (1976). The first appearance of obsidian in the cave is mentioned by Perlès (1979) and by Jacobsen and Van Horn (1974).

The reversal of opinion about hunter-gatherer life has been engagingly described by Sahlins (1972). For a general overview of Greece in the Stone Age, see Weinberg (1970). The many excavations and survey finds of Palaeolithic remains in Epiros (northwest Greece) are summarized in Coles and Higgs (1969: 311–27) and in Bailey et al. (1983a, 1983b). The sites on the island of Kefallinia are reported in Kavvadias (1984). The Mesolithic site of Sidhari, on Corfu, has been described by the excavator (Sordinas, 1970). A new and interesting account of Europe as a whole in the Stone Age by Robin Dennell (1983) includes a useful discussion of the important place Franchthi cave has in European archaeology.

Chapter 4 An Outpost of the Agricultural Revolution

With the onset of the Neolithic, the climate in the southern Argolid became like it is now or was perhaps a little more moist, and the landscape was at least in part covered with a deciduous oak parkland, if we may judge from pollen data from Thessaly (Bottema, 1979) and from Boeotia (Turner and Greig, 1975) and, for the latest Neolithic and the Bronze Age and beyond, from pollen records from the area itself (Sheehan, 1979) and from the western Peloponnese (Wright, 1972). Evidence for cultivated plants comes from the paleobotanical studies of cave deposits by Hansen (1980, and forthcoming), while the bone material (Payne, 1975, 1985) demonstrates the introduction of domesticated animals. The coastal evolution and its resources have been examined by Shackleton and van Andel (1980,

1986). The presence of submarine springs near the cave was known to the excavators (Jacobsen, 1973a, 1973b, 1981); they were found to be common in the area by van Andel and Lianos (1983). The Franchthi springs may have been one of the reasons for the settlement and its open air counterpart, now submerged (Gifford, 1983), and they may have provided the water for a small scale but reliable spring-fed agriculture similar to that practiced in Natufian Jericho (Hopf, 1969; Sherratt, 1980b).

The evidence for the Neolithic in Greece has been summarized by Dennell (1983), Mellaart (1975: 244–62), and especially Weinberg (1970). The period is more fully covered in a magnificently illustrated volume edited by D. Theocharis (1973). Jacobsen (1981) described the earliest Neolithic at Franchthi.

For trade in Neolithic Greece, see Renfrew (1973) and Runnels (1983b). N. J. Shackleton and Colin Renfrew (1970) documented the trade of *Spondylus* fragments to Europe, a subject now being extensively researched by Judith Shackleton (personal communication, 1986). The subject of trade links fostered by transhumant shepherds, or perhaps by women potters going to new homes in distant villages, is treated by Jacobsen (1984) and Vitelli (1974). The Neolithic of the Cycladic sites is discussed by Evans and Renfrew (1968) and Cherry and Torrence (1982). Cherry (1981) discusses the cause of the late date for colonization of the smaller islands.

Chapter 5   Civilization Coming

The soils and alluvia of the southern Argolid have been dealt with by Pope and van Andel (1984); further references to soils and soil erosion are given below for Chapter 8. The intermittent references to pollen records of lagoons are based on Sheehan (1979) and on Sheehan and Whitehead (1981).

Colin Renfrew's book (1972) is still the best, most innovative and thought-provoking work on the subject of the Aegean in the third millennium B.C. The dependence of the Early Bronze Age farmers on the availability of good arable land and their use for the first time of plows and draft animals to work the soil are discussed by Bintliff (1977) and by Sherratt (1980a). For wells in the Ermionis, see Harper (1976). Final Neolithic wells dating to the fourth millennium B.C. were found in the excavations of the Athenian Agora (Immerwahr, 1971: 1–21). The question of the Early Bronze Age shift to the south is discussed in detail by Renfrew (1972: 225–307), and briefly but more recently by Runnels (1985). Halstead (1977) describes the adjustments of settlement in Thessaly that took place at the same time. The comparative study of monumental buildings such as the House of Tiles at Lerna (Caskey, 1960) has only just begun (see Pullen, 1985; Themelis, 1984), but ultimately they will probably be considered houses for important families or persons. The wave of destruction that overwhelmed many islands and parts of central Greece and the northeastern Peloponnese is discussed by Caskey (1960) and in a series of papers dealing with the evidence from the pottery by Rutter (1979, 1983, 1984; see also Warren, 1980).

Useful overviews of the Peloponnese under the Mycenaeans are found in Chadwick (1976), Taylour (1983), Vermeule (1964), and Hope Simpson (1981). As for olives, even the Mycenaeans probably made more use of the wild than of the domesticated fruit, producing oil mainly to make scented unguents and perfumes, an industry requiring very few trees (Melena, 1983). A picture of provincial villages in the Bronze Age, in contrast to the excavations at the great palaces, is given by Blegen's excavations at Zygouries (1928), in the Korinthia, and by those of Mylonas at Ayios Kosmas (1959).

The problem of the Sea People and the new wave of destruction that ended the Bronze Age in the eastern Mediterranean has been treated thoroughly by Sandars (1978). Many hypotheses have been advanced for the causes of the fall of the Mycenaean empire, among them drought (Carpenter, 1966), civil war and revolution, volcanic eruption, an invasion of northern nomads (the Dorians), or just plain economic collapse. We shall steer clear of this debate, which, in some ways, has become a cottage industry. For brief, clear-headed summaries of the problem, see Chadwick (1976), Taylour (1983), and Sandars (1978).

Chapter 6   At the Edge of a Greater World

As before, discussions of soils and soil erosion are based mainly on Pope and van Andel (1984; see also references for Chapter 8), and the pollen data are from Sheehan (1979) and Sheehan and Whitehead (1981).

Among the many works available on early Greece we find Snodgrass (1971, 1980), Murray (1980), and Coldstream (1977) very useful. Boardman (1980) covers the phenomenon of Greek colonization, which may have included the southern Argolid. The Boeotian survey (Bintliff and Snodgrass, 1985) has documented similar growth in the

Classical period. We presume that the farmsteads with their towers were like those described from Attica by Young (1956) and Pečirka (1973), or like the one fully excavated at Vari, in Attica (Jones et al., 1973).

For the production of olive oil in Classical and Roman times, see Forbes and Foxhall (1976) and Drachmann (1932). Most of our knowledge about olives in ancient Greece comes from representations on painted vases or from finds of olive crushers and presses. Boardman (1977) discusses the use of olive oil in ancient Greece for eating, bathing, lighting, and industry. Even when economically important, however, the quantities used were probably small. Boardman illustrates, for example, a small painted vase that shows two men filling a tiny jar with olive oil and above them an inscription that reads, "Oh Father Zeus, let me grow rich!" We are reminded here that the oil, often scented, was used in Classical and Roman times for body ointment or in place of soap, much as in the later Bronze Age. Its manufacture and sale were an important industry for some regions.

For the decline in population and the depressed economy of the later Hellenistic and early Roman era, see Rostovtzeff (1941), Larsen (1938), and Tarn and Griffith (1952). By the mid-third century B.C. and on through the Hellenistic era, Greek families, as is known from historians and inscriptions, often counted only one child, almost always male. Indeed, the imbalance of sons to daughters clearly confirms the ancient practice of female infanticide attested by the historians; and senilicide, the killing of old people, is also likely (Tarn and Griffith, 1952: 100–104; see also Camp, 1979). Wars, first those of the Successors of Alexander, then the Roman civil wars of the first century B.C., and—last but not least—the civil anarchy and barbarian invasions of the third century A.D., were also responsible for considerable depopulation. Piracy was a constant threat both to seaborne commerce and to coastal settlements, which were raided for slaves (Ormerod, 1978).

The Late Roman decline is briefly described by Gregory (1982) and Cheetham (1981); more detailed accounts can be found in the well known histories of the period. Outdated but still magnificent is Edward Gibbon's *Decline and Fall of the Roman Empire*. Interesting reading is also Vasiliev (1952). In the late sixth century the population decline in Greece may have been hastened by the ravages of bubonic plague (see McNeill, 1976: 109–31), a recurrent problem.

The excavation of the rustic villa at Halieis has been reported by Rudolph (1979). Frost (1977) describes a similar establishment farther up the east coast of the Argolid toward Poros, and now under 2 m of water. The exploration of Ermioni has been largely unpublished, and we have relied upon Michael Jameson for the identification of visible antiquities. For Late Roman pottery production in the Argolid, see Megaw and Jones (1983).

Chapter 7 *Byzantine Chapels to Beach Hotels*

For soils see Pope and van Andel (1984) and references for Chapter 8; for pollen data see Sheehan (1979) and Sheehan and Whitehead (1981).

The invasions of Greece by barbarians and the disruptions they caused are described briefly in Gregory (1982) and at greater length by Cheetham (1981), Vasiliev (1952), and Vlasto (1970). For the history of Thermisi castle and an outline of the later political history of the Argolid, see McLeod (1962) and Topping (1976; and in Sutton, forthcoming). Cheetham (1981) provides a concise overview of medieval Greece. The early modern economy of the region is a big subject, but a start may be made with Jameson (1976) and other excellent papers in Dimen and Friedl (1976), and, shortly, those brought together by Sutton (forthcoming).

Chapter 8 *Learning to Take Care of the Soil*

The processes of soil formation have been described by Birkeland (1984: 118–52), Leeder (1975), and Wieder and Yaalon (1982). Details regarding the evolution of soils and the use of soil maturity for stratigraphic correlations and age estimates are given by Birkeland (1984: 194–224), by Harden (1982), and by Morrison (1976). The B horizon, with its clays, and the calcareous horizon underneath have been described by Birkeland (1984: 194–224; see also Harden, 1982; Morrison, 1976).

The model currently in wide use for late Quaternary alluviation history in the Mediterranean was conceived by Vita-Finzi (1969) and much promulgated by Bintliff (1975, 1977). Contrary evidence and recent criticism can be found in, for example, studies by Drost (1974), Eisma (1964), Davidson (1980), Raphael (1973), Paepe et al. (1980), Pope and van Andel (1984), and especially Wagstaff (1981). See also van Andel et al. (1986).

Regarding the deposition of various types of alluvium, our interpretation rests on a large body of literature for which Picard and

High (1973) and Patton and Schumm (1981) provide good summaries. Bull (1972, 1977), Hooke (1967), and Innes (1983) deal with debris flows; Rust (1978) and Miall (1977), with streamflood deposits and the braided stream regime. Naveh and Dan (1973) and Rackham (1983) discuss the role of natural vegetation and its recolonization of deserted lands. Gophna (1979) refers to the introduction of slope terraces in the Levant, and Donkin (1979) provides comparative data from Central and South America on terracing for control of soil erosion. Butzer (1980) and Ku et al. (1979) discuss dating techniques for alluvia and soils, and Bell (1982) and Butzer (1974) consider the role of human land use in soil erosion and valley alluviation. A more complete overview of the literature is given in Pope and van Andel (1984) and van Andel et al. (1986).

Chapter 9   *Growth and Decline: A History of People*

For a discussion of the myriad problems in interpreting archaeological data that have been subjected to countless natural and cultural forces before ending up on the surface to be found by the surveying archaeologist, see Schiffer (1976) and Murray and Kardulias (1986). An account of the settlement history of the southern Argolid has been prepared by Runnels and van Andel (1987), and full details for all sites are to be given in a site register in Jameson et al. (forthcoming).

For a general outline of the development of the early polis, see Snodgrass (1980). The Archaic sanctuary at Halieis has been described by Jameson (1974). The burials at Franchthi cave have been treated in detail by Jacobsen and Cullen (1981), and those at Halieis by Dengate (1980). For wells and water supplies, see Harper (1976).

The surveys in Greece that turned up the alternating settlement patterns described here have been discussed by Bintliff (1977), Bintliff and Snodgrass (1985), McDonald and Rapp (1972), and Renfrew and Wagstaff (1982). For the overall demographic picture of modern Greece and the Ermionis we are once again indebted to the papers in Dimen and Friedl (1976) and to Susan B. Sutton, who has shared her preliminary findings regarding the demographic history of the area with us (see also Sutton, forthcoming).

The population of the medieval and modern Ermionis has been estimated following Topping (1972, 1976), with judicious use of statistics from the Greek National Statistics Service. Guesses about the Bronze Age population are based on cemetery data of contemporary sites outside the Argolid, using a method outlined by Wells (1984) and Hassan (1981). For the Bronze Age and following periods we have assigned population density figures based on site areas. Jacobsen (1981) estimated a probable density of about 100 persons per hectare for Neolithic villages in Greece, while for the built-up area of the towns (poleis) Pounds (1969) used 150 persons per hectare. Other population estimates, based, for example, on the productive capabilities of arable land with primitive technology, or on historical records, are even more difficult to make, and even more uncertain. For attempts to make the complex and uncertain calculations for population in the Classical period, see Jameson (1976), Bintliff and Snodgrass (1985), and Pounds (1969).

Bibliography

Bachmann, G. H., and H. Risch. 1978. Late Mesozoic and Paleogene development of the Argolid peninsula (Peloponnesos). In *Alps, Apennines, Hellenides*, edited by H. Closs, D. Roeder, and K. Schmidt, 424–27. Interunion Geodynamics Commission, Scientific Reports, 38. Stuttgart.

———. 1979. Die geologische Entwicklung der Argolis-Halbinsel (Peloponnes, Griechenland). *Geologisches Jahrbuch*, ser. B, 32, 3–177.

Bailey, G. N., P. L. Carter, C. S. Gamble, and H. N. Higgs. 1983a. Epirus revisited: Seasonality and inter-site variation in the Upper Palaeolithic of northwest Greece. In *Hunter-Gatherer Economy in Prehistory*, edited by G. N. Bailey, 64–78. Cambridge.

———. 1983b. Asprochaliko and Kastritsa: Further investigations of Palaeolithic settlement and economy in Epirus (northwest Greece). *Proceedings of the Prehistoric Society*, 49, 15–42.

Bannert, D., and H. Bender. 1968. Zur Geologie der Argolid Halbinsel, Peloponnes, Griechenland. *Geologica et Palaeontologica*, 2, 151–62.

Bell, M. 1982. The effects of land-use and climate on valley sedimentation. In *Climatic Change in Later Prehistory*, edited by A. Harding, 127–42. Edinburgh.

Bialor, P., and M. H. Jameson. 1962. Palaeolithic in the Argolid. *American Journal of Archaeology*, 66, 181–82.

Bintliff, J. L. 1975. Sediments and settlement in southern Greece. In *Geoarchaeology*, edited by D. A. Davidson and M. L. Shackley, 267–75. London.

———. 1977. *Natural Environment and Human Settlement in Prehistoric Greece*. British Archaeological Reports, Supplementary Series, 28. Oxford.

Bintliff, J. L., and A. M. Snodgrass. 1985. The Cambridge/Bradford Boeotian Expedition. *Journal of Field Archaeology*, 12, 123–63.

Birkeland, P. W. 1984. *Soils and Geomorphology*. Oxford.

Blegen, C. W. 1928. *Zygouries: A Prehistoric Settlement in the Valley of Cleonae*. Cambridge, Mass.

Boardman, J. 1977. The olive in the Mediterranean: Its culture and use. In *The Early History of Agriculture*, edited by J. Hutchinson, 187–96. Oxford.

————. 1980. *The Greeks Overseas*. London.

Bottema, S. 1979. Pollen analytical investigations in Thessaly, Greece. *Palaeohistoria*, 21, 19–40.

Boyd, T. D., and W. W. Rudolph. 1978. Excavations at Porto Cheli and vicinity, preliminary report IV: The lower town of Halieis. *Hesperia*, 47, 333–55.

Bull, W. B. 1972. Recognition of alluvial-fan deposits in the stratigraphic record. In *Recognition of Ancient Sedimentary Environments*, edited by K. J. Rigby and W. K. Hamblin, 68–83. Society of Economic Paleontologists and Mineralogists, Special Publication 16. Tulsa, Okla.

————. 1977. The alluvial fan environment. *Progress in Physical Geography*, 1, 130–48.

Butzer, K. W. 1974. Accelerated soil erosion: A problem of man-land relationships. In *Perspectives on Environment*, edited by I. R. Manners and M. Mikesell, 57–78. Association of American Geographers, Commission on College Geography, Publication 13. Washington, D.C.

————. 1980. Holocene alluvial sequences: Problems of dating and correlation. In *Timescales in Geomorphology*, edited by R. A. Cullingford, D. A. Davidson, and J. Lewin, 131–42. New York.

————. 1982. *Archaeology as Human Ecology*. Cambridge.

Camp, J. 1979. A drought in the late eighth century B.C. *Hesperia*, 48, 397–411.

Carpenter, R. 1966. *Discontinuity in Greek Civilization*. Cambridge.

Caskey, J. L. 1960. The Early Helladic period in the Argolid. *Hesperia*, 29, 285–303.

Chadwick, J. 1976. *The Mycenaean World*. Cambridge.

Cheetham, N. 1981. *Mediaeval Greece*. New Haven, Conn.

Cherry, J. F. 1981. Pattern and process in the earliest colonisation of the Mediterranean islands. *Proceedings of the Prehistoric Society*, 47, 41–68.

Cherry, J. F., and R. Torrence. 1982. The earliest prehistory of Melos. In *An Island Polity: The Archaeology of Exploitation in Melos*, edited by C. Renfrew and J. M. Wagstaff, 24–34. Cambridge.

Clark-Forbes, M. H. 1976. Farming and foraging in prehistoric Greece: A cultural ecological perspective. In *Regional Variation in Modern Greece and Cyprus*, edited by M. Dimen and E. Friedl, 127–42. Annals of the New York Academy of Sciences, 268. New York.

Coldstream, N. 1977. *Geometric Greece*. London.

Coles, J. M., and E. S. Higgs. 1969. *The Archaeology of Man*. Harmondsworth.

Davidson, D. A. 1980. Erosion in Greece during the first and second millennia B.C. In *Timescales in Geomorphology*, edited by R. A. Cullingford, D. A. Davidson, and J. Lewin, 143–58. New York.

Dengate, C. 1980. A group of graves excavated at Halieis. *Archaiologikou Deltiou Chronika*, 31, 274–324.

Dennell, R. 1983. *European Economic Prehistory: A New Approach*. London.

Dimen, M., and E. Friedl, eds. 1976. *Regional Variation in Modern Greece and Cyprus: Toward a Perspective on the Ethnography of Greece*. Annals of the New York Academy of Sciences, 268. New York.

Donkin, R. A. 1979. *Agricultural Terracing in the Aboriginal New World*. Viking Fund Publications in Anthropology, 56. Tucson, Ariz.

Drachmann, A. G. 1932. *Ancient Oil Mills and Presses*. Det Kgl. Videnskabernes Selskab, Archaeologiske-Kunsthistoriske Meddelelser, 1. Copenhagen.

Drost, B. W. 1974. Late Quaternary stratigraphy of the southern Argolid. M.S. thesis, University of Pennsylvania. Philadelphia.

Dyson, S. 1982. Archaeological survey in the Mediterranean basin: A review of recent research. *American Antiquity*, 47, 87–98.

Eisma, D. 1964. Stream deposition in the Mediterranean area in historical times. *Nature*, 203, 1061–62.

Evans, J. D., and C. Renfrew. 1968. *Excavations at Saliagos near Antiparos*. London.

Flemming, N. C. 1968. Holocene earth movements and eustatic sea level change in the Peloponnese. *Nature*, 217, 1031–32.

Forbes, H. A. 1982. Strategies and soils: Technology, production and the environment in the peninsula of Methana, Greece. Ph.D. dissertation, University of Pennsylvania Philadelphia.

Forbes, H. A., and L. Foxhall. 1976. The "Queen of all Trees": Preliminary notes on the archaeology of the olive. *Expedition*, 21, 37–47.

Forbes, H. A., and H. A. Koster. 1976. Fire, axe, and plow: Human influence on local plant communities in the southern Argolid. In *Regional Variation in Modern Greece and Cyprus*, edited by M. Dimen and E. Friedl, 109–26. Annals of the New York Academy of Sciences, 268. New York.

Frost, F. J. 1977. Phourkari: A villa complex in the Argolid (Greece). *International Journal of Nautical Archaeology and Underwater Exploration*, 6, 233–38.

Gavrielides, N. E. 1976. The impact of olive growing on the landscape of the Fournoi valley. In *Regional Variation in Modern Greece and Cyprus*, edited by M. Dimen and E. Friedl, 143–57. Annals of the New York Academy of Sciences, 268. New York.

Gifford, J. A. 1983. Core sampling of a Holocene marine sequence and underlying Neolithic cultural material off Franchthi cave. In *Quaternary Coastlines and Marine Archaeology*, edited by P. M. Masters and N. C. Flemming, 269–81. New York.

Gophna, R. 1979. Post-Neolithic settlement patterns. In *The Quaternary of Israel*, edited by A. Horowitz, 319–21. New York.

Gregory, T. 1982. The fortified cities of Greece. *Archaeology*, 35, 14–21.

Halstead, P. 1977. Prehistoric Thessaly: The submergence of civilisation. In *Mycenaean Geography*, edited by J. L. Bintliff, 23–29. Cambridge.

Hansen, J. M. 1980. The paleoethnobotany of Franchthi cave, Greece. Ph.D. dissertation, University of Minnesota. Minneapolis.

———. Forthcoming. The paleoethnobotany of Franchthi cave. In *Excavations at Franchthi Cave, Greece*, edited by T. W. Jacobsen. Bloomington, Ind.

Harden, J. W. 1982. A quantitative index of soil development from field descriptions: Examples from a chronosequence in central California. *Geoderma*, 28, 1–28.

Harper, D. B. 1976. Just add water. . . . *Expedition*, 19, 40–49.

Hassan, F. 1981. *Demographic Archaeology*. New York.

Hooke, R. L. 1967. Processes on arid region alluvial fans. *Journal of Geology*, 75, 438–60.

Hope Simpson, R. 1981. *Mycenaean Greece*. Park Ridge, N.J.

Hopf, M. 1969. Plant remains and early farming in Jericho. In *The Domestication and Exploitation of Plants and Animals*, edited by P. Ucko and G. Dimbleby, 355–60. London.

Hughes, J. D. 1983. How the ancients viewed deforestation. *Journal of Field Archaeology*, 10, 437–45.

Immerwahr, S. A. 1971. *The Neolithic and Bronze Ages.* The Athenian Agora, 13. Princeton, N.J.

Innes, J. L. 1983. Debris flows. *Progress in Physical Geography*, 7, 469–501.

Jacobsen, T. W. 1969. Excavations at Porto Cheli and vicinity, preliminary report II: The Franchthi cave, 1967–1968. *Hesperia*, 38, 343–81.

————. 1973a. Excavations in the Franchthi cave, 1969–1971, part I. *Hesperia*, 42, 45–88.

————. 1973b. Excavations in the Franchthi cave, 1969–1971, part II. *Hesperia*, 42, 253–83.

————. 1976. 17,000 years of Greek prehistory. *The Scientific American*, 234, 76–87.

————. 1979. Excavations at Franchthi cave, 1973–1979. *Archaiologikou Deltiou Chronika*, 29, 268–82.

————. 1981. Franchthi cave and the beginning of settled village life in Greece. *Hesperia*, 50, 303–19.

————. 1984. Seasonal pastoralism in southern Greece: A consideration of the ecology of Neolithic Urfirnis pottery. In *Pots and Potters: Current Approaches in Ceramic Archaeology*, edited by P. M. Rice, 27–43. University of California at Los Angeles, Institute of Archaeology, Monograph 24. Los Angeles.

————, ed. Forthcoming. *Excavations at Franchthi Cave, Greece.* Bloomington, Ind.

Jacobsen, T. W., and C. Cullen. 1981. A consideration of mortuary practices in Neolithic Greece: Burials from Franchthi cave. In *Mortality and Immortality: The Anthropology of Death*, edited by S. C. Humphreys and H. King, 79–101. London.

Jacobsen, T. W., and D. M. Van Horn. 1974. The Franchthi cave flint survey: Some preliminary results (1974). *Journal of Field Archaeology*, 1, 305–8.

Jameson, M. H. 1969. Excavations at Porto Cheli and vicinity, preliminary report I: Halieis, 1962–1968. *Hesperia*, 38, 311–42.

————. 1974. The excavation of a drowned Greek temple. *The Scientific American*, 231, 110–19.

————. 1976. The southern Argolid: The setting for historical and cultural studies. In *Regional Variation in Modern Greece and Cyprus*, edited by M. Dimen and E. Friedl, 74–91. Annals of the New York Academy of Sciences, 268. New York.

Jameson, M. H., C. N. Runnels, and Tj. H. van Andel. Forthcoming. *A Greek Countryside: The Southern Argolid from Prehistory to the Present Day.* Stanford, Calif.

Jones, J. E., A. J. Grahm, and L. H. Sackett. 1973. *An Attic Country House below the Cave of Pan at Vari.* London.

Kavvadias, G. 1984. *Palaiolithiki Kephalonia: O Politismos tou Phiskardhou.* (Palaeolithic Kefallinia: The Fiskardhou Culture.) Athens.

Keller, D. R., and D. W. Rupp, eds. 1983. *Archaeological Survey in the Mediterranean Area.* British Archaeological Reports, International Series, 155. Oxford.

Koster, H. A., and J. B. Koster. 1976. Competition or symbiosis?: Pastoral adaptive strategies in the southern Argolid. In *Regional Variation in Modern Greece and Cyprus,* edited by M. Dimen and E. Friedl, 275–85. Annals of the New York Academy of Sciences, 268. New York.

Ku, T.-L., W. B. Bull, S. T. Freeman, and K. G. Knauss. 1979. 230-Th/234-U dating of pedogenic carbonates in gravelly desert soils of Vidal Valley, southeastern California. *Bulletin of the Geological Society of America,* 90, 1063–73.

Lamb, H. H. 1982. *Climate History and the Modern World.* London.

Larsen, J. A. O. 1938. Roman Greece. In *An Economic Survey of Ancient Rome,* edited by T. Frank, 4, 259–499. Baltimore.

Leeder, M. R. 1975. Pedogenic carbonates and flood sediment accretion rates: A quantitative model for alluvial arid zone lithofacies. *Geological Magazine,* 112, 257–70.

McDonald, W. A., and G. R. Rapp, eds. 1972. *The Minnesota Messenia Expedition: Reconstructing a Bronze Age Regional Environment.* Minneapolis.

McLeod, W. E. 1962. Kiveri and Thermisi. *Hesperia,* 31, 378–92.

McNeill, W. H. 1976. *Plagues and People.* Garden City, N.Y.

Megaw, A., and R. Jones. 1983. Byzantine and allied pottery: A contribution by chemical analysis to problems of origin and distribution. *The Annual of the British School at Athens,* 78, 235–63.

Meiggs, R. 1982. *Trees and Timber in the Ancient Mediterranean World.* Oxford.

Melena, J. L. 1983. Olive oil and other sorts of oil in the Mycenaean tablets. *Minos,* 18, 89–123.

Mellaart, J. 1975. *The Neolithic of the Near East.* London.

Miall, A. D. 1977. A review of the braided river depositional environment. *Earth Science Reviews,* 13, 1–62.

Morrison, R. B. 1976. Quaternary soil stratigraphic concepts, methods, and problems. In *Quaternary Soils: Papers from the 3rd Symposium on Quaternary Research*, edited by W. C. Mahaney, 77–108. Norwich, Eng.

Murray, O. 1980. *Early Greece*. Atlantic Highlands, N.J.

Murray, P., and P. N. Kardulias. 1986. A modern site survey in the southern Argolid, Greece. *Journal of Field Archaeology*, 13, 20–41.

Mylonas, G. E. 1959. *Aghios Kosmas: An Early Bronze Age Settlement and Cemetery in Attica*. Princeton, N.J.

Naveh, Z., and J. Dan. 1973. The human degradation of Mediterranean landscapes in Israel. In *Mediterranean Type Ecosystems: Origin and Structure*, edited by F. Castri and H. A. Mooney, 373–90. New York.

NID. 1944. *Greece: Physical Geography, History, Administration, and Peoples*. Naval Intelligence Division, Geographical Handbook BR 516, I, 166–69. London.

Ormerod, H. A. 1978. *Piracy in the Ancient World*. Totowa, N.J.

Paepe, R., M. E. Hatziotis, and J. Thorez. 1980. *Geomorphological Evolution of the Eastern Mediterranean Belt and Mesopotamian Plain*. International Geological Correlation Programme, Project 146: River Flood and Lake Level Changes. Paris.

Patton, P. C., and S. A. Schumm. 1981. Ephemeral stream processes: Implications for studies of Quaternary valley fills. *Quaternary Research*, 15, 24–43.

Payne, S. 1975. Faunal change at Franchthi cave from 20,000 B.C.–3000 B.C. In *Archaeozoological Studies*, edited by A. T. Clason, 120–31. Amsterdam.

———. 1982. Faunal evidence for environmental/climatic change at Franchthi cave (southern Argolid, Greece), 25,000 B.P.–5,000 B.P.: Preliminary results. In *Palaeoclimates, Palaeoenvironments and Human Communities in the Eastern Mediterranean Region in Later Prehistory*, edited by J. L. Bintliff and W. van Zeist, 133–37. British Archaeological Reports, International Series, 133. Oxford.

———. 1985. Zoo-archaeology in Greece: A reader's guide. In *Contributions to Aegean Archaeology: Studies in Honor of William A. McDonald*, edited by N. C. Wilkie and W. D. Coulson, 211–44. Dubuque, Iowa.

Pečirka, J. 1973. Homestead farms in Classical and Hellenistic Hellas. In *Problèmes de la terre en Grèce ancienne*, edited by M. I. Finley, 113–47. The Hague.

Perlès, C. 1979. Des navigateurs méditerranéens il y a 10,000 ans. *La Recherche*, 96, 82–83.

———. Forthcoming. Présentation générale et industries paléolithiques: Les industries lithiques taillées de Franchthi. In *Excavations at Franchthi Cave, Greece*, edited by T. W. Jacobsen. Bloomington, Ind.

Perry, W. R. 1981. Mediterranean climate: A synoptic appraisal. *Progress in Physical Geography*, 5, 107–13.

Peterson, G. M., T. Webb III, J. E. Kutzbach, T. van der Hammen, T. Wijmstra, and F. A. Street. 1979. The continental record of environmental conditions at 18,000 yr B.P.: An initial evaluation. *Quaternary Research*, 12, 47–82.

Picard, M. D., and L. R. High. 1973. *Sedimentary Structures of Ephemeral Streams*. Amsterdam.

Pope, K. O., C. N. Runnels, and T.-L. Ku. 1984. Dating Middle Palaeolithic redbeds in southern Greece. *Nature*, 312, 264–66.

Pope, K. O., and Tj. H. van Andel. 1984. Late Quaternary alluviation and soil formation in the southern Argolid: Its history, causes and archaeological implications. *Journal of Archaeological Science*, 11, 281–306.

Poulianos, A. 1981. Pre-*sapiens* man in Greece. *Current Anthropology*, 22, 287–88.

Pounds, N. J. G. 1969. The urbanization of the Classical world. *Annals of the Association of American Geographers*, 59, 135–57.

Pullen, D. J. 1985. Social organization in Early Bronze Age Greece: A multi-dimensional approach. Ph.D. dissertation, Indiana University. Bloomington.

Rackham, O. 1983. Observations on the historical ecology of Boeotia. *The Annual of the British School at Athens*, 78, 291–351.

Raphael, C. N. 1973. Late Quaternary changes in coastal Elis, Greece. *Geographical Review*, 63, 73–89.

Renfrew, C. 1972. *The Emergence of Civilisation: The Cyclades and the Aegean in the Third Millennium B.C.* London.

———. 1973. Trade and craft specialization. In *Neolithic Greece*, edited by D. Theocharis, 179–200. Athens.

Renfrew, C., and J. M. Wagstaff, eds. 1982. *An Island Polity: The Archaeology of Exploitation in Melos*. Cambridge.

Rostovtzeff, M. 1941. *The Social and Economic History of the Hellenistic World*. Oxford.

Rudolph, W. W. 1979. Excavations at Porto Cheli and vicinity, preliminary report V: The early Byzantine remains. *Hesperia*, 48, 294–324.

———. 1984. Excavations at Porto Cheli and vicinity, preliminary report VI: Halieis, the stratigraphy of the streets in the northeast quarter of the lower town. *Hesperia*, 53, 123–70.

Runnels, C. N. 1983a. The Stanford University archaeological and environmental survey of the southern Argolid, Greece: 1979–1981. In *Archaeological Survey in the Mediterranean Area*, eited by D. R. Keller and D. W. Rupp, 261–63. British Archaeological Reports, International Series, 155. Oxford.

———. 1983b. Trade and communication in prehistoric Greece. *Ekistics: The Problems and Science of Human Settlements*, 50, 417–20.

———. 1985. Trade and the demand for millstones in southern Greece in the Neolithic and the Early Bronze Age. In *Prehistoric Production and Exchange: The Aegean and Eastern Mediterranean*, edited by B. Knapp and T. Stech, 30–43. University of California at Los Angeles, Institute of Archaeology, Monograph 25. Los Angeles.

Runnels, C. N., and Tj. H. van Andel. 1987. Archaeological evidence for settlement patterns in the southern Argolid, Greece. *Hesperia*, 56, in press.

Rust, B. R. 1978. Depositional models for braided alluvium. In *Fluvial Sedimentology*, edited by A. D. Miall, 605–25. Canadian Society of Petroleum Geologists, Memoir 5. Calgary, Alta.

Rutter, J. B. 1979. *Ceramic Change in the Aegean Early Bronze Age. The Kastri Group, Lefkandi I, and Lerna IV: A Theory Concerning the Origin of Early Helladic III Ceramics*. University of California at Los Angeles, Institute of Archaeology, Occasional Papers, 5. Los Angeles.

———. 1983. Fine gray-burnished pottery of the Early Helladic III period: The ancestry of Gray Minyan. *Hesperia*, 52, 327–55.

———. 1984. The "Early Cycladic III gap": What it is and how to go about filling it without making it go away. In *The Prehistoric Cyclades: Contributions to a Workshop on Cycladic Chronology*, edited by J. A. MacGillivray and R. L. N. Barber, 95–107. Edinburgh.

Sahlins, M. 1972. *Stone Age Economics*. New York.

Sandars, N. K. 1978. *The Sea Peoples*. London.

Schiffer, M. 1976. *Behavioral Archaeology*. New York.

Shackleton, J. C. In press. Reconstructing past shorelines as an approach to determining factors affecting shellfish collecting in the prehistoric past. In *Coastal Archaeology*, edited by G. N. Bailey and J. Parkington. Cambridge.

Shackleton, J. C., and Tj. H. van Andel. 1980. Prehistoric shell assemblages from Franchthi cave and the evolution of the adjacent coastal zone. *Nature*, 288, 357–59.

———. 1986. Prehistoric shore environments, shellfish availability, and shellfish gathering at Franchthi, Greece. *International Journal of Geoarchaeology*, 1, 127–43.

Shackleton, N. J., and C. Renfrew. 1970. Neolithic trade routes realigned by oxygen isotope analysis. *Nature*, 228, 1062–65.

Sheehan, M. C. 1979. The post-glacial vegetational history of the southern Argolid, Greece. Ph.D. dissertation, Indiana University. Bloomington.

Sheehan, M. C., and D. R. Whitehead. 1981. The late-postglacial vegetational history of the Argolid peninsula, Greece. *National Geographic Society Research Reports*, 13, 693–708.

Sherratt, A. G. 1980a. Early agricultural communities in Europe. In *The Cambridge Encyclopedia of Archaeology*, edited by A. G. Sherratt and G. Clark, 144–51. Cambridge.

———. 1980b. Water, soil and seasonality in early cereal cultivation. *World Archaeology*, 11, 313–30.

Snodgrass, A. M. 1971. *The Dark Age of Greece*. Edinburgh.

———. 1980. *Archaic Greece: The Age of Experiment*. Berkeley and Los Angeles.

Sordinas, A. 1970. *Stone Implements from Northwestern Corfu, Greece*. Memphis State University, Anthropological Research Center, Occasional Papers, 4. Memphis, Tenn.

Stringer, C. B., F. C. Howell, and J. K. Melentis. 1979. The significance of the fossil hominid skull from Petralona, Greece. *Journal of Archaeological Science*, 6, 295–98.

Süsskoch, H. 1967. Die Geologie der südöstlichen Argolis (Peloponnes, Griechenland). Ph.D. dissertation, University of Marburg. Marburg, Germany.

Sutton, S. B., ed. Forthcoming. *Shepherds, Farmers, and Sailors: Economy and Regional Development in the Argolid Peninsula*. Stanford, Calif.

Tarn, W. W., and G. T. Griffith. 1952. *Hellenistic Civilisation*. 3d ed., revised. London.

Taylour, W. B. 1983. *The Mycenaeans*. London.

Themelis, P. 1984. Early Helladic monumental architecture. *Mitteilungen des Deutschen archäologischen Instituts in Athen*, 99, 335–51.

Theocharis, D., ed. 1973. *Neolithic Greece*. Athens.

Tollner, H. 1976. Zum Klima von Griechenland. *Beiträge zur Landeskunde Griechenlands*, 6, 267–81.

Topping, P. 1972. The post-Classical documents. In *The Minnesota Messenia Expedition: Reconstructing a Bronze Age Regional Environment*, edited by W. A. McDonald and G. R. Rapp, 64–80. Minneapolis.

———. 1976. Premodern Peloponnesus: The land and the people under Venetian rule (1685–1715). In *Regional Variation in Modern Greece and Cyprus*, edited by M. Dimen and E. Friedl, 92–108. Annals of the New York Academy of Sciences, 268. New York.

Turner, J., and J. R. A. Greig. 1975. Some Holocene pollen diagrams from Greece. *Review of Palaeobotany and Palynology*, 20, 171–204.

van Andel, Tj. H., and N. Lianos. 1983. Prehistoric and historic shorelines of the southern Argolid peninsula: A subbottom profiler study. *International Journal of Nautical Archaeology and Underwater Exploration*, 12, 303–24.

———. 1984. High-resolution seismic reflection profiles for the reconstruction of post-glacial transgressive shorelines: An example from Greece. *Quaternary Research*, 22, 31–45.

van Andel, Tj. H., C. N. Runnels, and K. O. Pope. 1986. Five thousand years of land use and abuse in the southern Argolid, Greece. *Hesperia*, 55, 103–28.

van Andel, Tj. H., and J. C. Shackleton. 1982. Late Paleolithic and Mesolithic coastlines of Greece and the Aegean. *Journal of Field Archaeology*, 9, 445–54.

van Andel, Tj. H., and S. B. Sutton. Forthcoming. Landscape and people of the Franchthi region. In *Excavations at Franchthi Cave, Greece*, edited by T. W. Jacobsen. Bloomington, Ind.

van Zeist, W., and S. Bottema. 1982. Vegetational history of the Mediterranean during the last 20,000 years. In *Palaeoclimates, Palaeoenvironments and Human Communities in the Eastern Mediterranean Region in Later Prehistory*, edited by J. L. Bintliff and W. van Zeist, 277–321. British Archaeological Reports, International Series, 133. Oxford.

Vasiliev, A. A. 1952. *History of the Byzantine Empire*. Madison, Wis.

Vermeule, E. 1964. *Greece in the Bronze Age*. Chicago.

Vita-Finzi, C. 1969. *The Mediterranean Valleys: Geological Change in Historical Time*. Cambridge.

Vitelli, K. D. 1974. The Greek Neolithic patterned Urfirnis ware from the Franchthi cave and Lerna. Ph.D. dissertation, University of Pennsylvania. Philadelphia.

Vlasto, A. P. 1970. *The Entry of the Slavs into Christendom*. Cambridge.

Vrielinck, B. 1982. Evolution paléogéographique et structurale de la presqu'île de l'Argolide (Grèce). *Revue de Géologie Dynamique et Géographie Physique*, 23, 277–88.

Wagstaff, J. M. 1981. Buried assumptions: Some problems in the interpretation of the "Younger Fill" raised by recent data from Greece. *Journal of Archaeological Science*, 8, 247–64.

Wagstaff, J. M., and J. F. Cherry. 1982. Settlement and population change. In *An Island Polity: The Archaeology of Exploitation in Melos*, edited by C. Renfrew and J. M. Wagstaff, 136–55. Cambridge.

Warren, P. 1980. Problems of chronology in Crete and the Aegean in the third and earlier second millennium B.C. *American Journal of Archaeology*, 84, 487–99.

Weinberg, S. S. 1970. The Stone Age in the Aegean. In *The Cambridge Ancient History*, I (1), 557–618. Cambridge.

Wells, P. S. 1984. *Farms, Villages, and Cities: Commerce and Urban Origins in Late Prehistoric Europe*. Ithaca, N.Y.

Wieder, M., and D. H. Yaalon. 1982. Micromorphological fabrics and developmental stages of carbonate nodular forms related to soil characteristics. *Geoderma*, 28, 203–20.

Wigley, T. M. L., and G. Farmer. 1982. Climate of the eastern Mediterranean and Near East. In *Palaeoclimates, Palaeoenvironments and Human Communities in the Eastern Mediterranean Region in Later Prehistory*, edited by J. M. Bintliff and W. van Zeist, 3–37. British Archaeological Reports, International Series, 133. Oxford.

Wintle, A. G., and J. A. Jacobs. 1982. A critical review of the dating evidence for Petralona cave. *Journal of Archaeological Science*, 9, 39–47.

Wright, H. E. 1972. Vegetational history. In *The Minnesota Messenia Expedition: Reconstructing a Bronze Age Regional Environment*, edited by W. A. McDonald and G. R. Rapp, 188–99. Minneapolis.

Young, J. H. 1956. Studies in south Attica. *Hesperia*, 25, 122–46.

Index

Library of Congress Cataloging-in-Publication Data

van Andel, Tjeerd H. (Tjeerd Hendrik), 1923–
  Beyond the Acropolis.
  Bibliography: p.
  Includes index.
    1. Greece—Rural conditions.   2. Greece—Social
life and customs.   I. Runnels, Curtis Neil,
1950–   . II. Title.
DF109.V36   1987   949.5   86-30047
ISBN 0-8047-1389-8 (alk. paper)